Howard W. Odum's Folklore Odyssey

# Howard W. Odum's Folklore Odyssey

*Transformation*

*to Tolerance*

*through*

*African American*

*Folk Studies*

LYNN MOSS SANDERS

The University of

Georgia Press

*Athens and London*

Acknowledgments for the use of copyrighted material
appear on page xvi, which constitutes an extension of
the copyright page.

Designed by Kathi Dailey Morgan
Set in Berthold Baskerville by Bookcomp, Inc.
Printed and bound by Thomson-Shore, Inc.
The paper in this book meets the guidelines for
permanence and durability of the Committee on
Production Guidelines for Book Longevity of the
Council on Library Resources.
Printed in the United States of America
07  06  05  04  03  C  5  4  3  2  1

Library of Congress Cataloging-in-Publication Data
Sanders, Lynn Moss.
Howard W. Odum's folklore odyssey : transformation
to tolerance through African American folk studies /
Lynn Moss Sanders.
p. cm.
Includes bibliographical references and index.
ISBN 0-8203-2549-X (hardcover : alk. paper)
Contents: African American folklore and Odum's
liberal agenda at the University of North Carolina–
Odum and Johnson's collaborative folk-song collections–
African American folklore in Odum's Black Ulysses trilogy–
Odum's literary collaboration with John Wesley Gordon–
Folklore and racial tolerance in the academy–
Mentoring and collaboration as keys to cultural
understanding.
1. Odum, Howard Washington, 1884–1954.
2. Folklorists–Southern States–Biography.
3. Sociologists–Southern States–Biography.
4. Authors, American–Biography.   5. African
Americans–Folklore.   6. African Americans–
Music–History and criticism.   7. Folk music–
Southern States–History and criticism.   8. Southern
States–Race relations.   I. Title.
GR55.O38 S36 2003
398'.092 B–dc21        2003011159
British Library Cataloging-in-Publication Data available

*In loving memory*

William Truett Moss

1/11/1932–11/1/2000

*"To strive, to seek, to find, and not to yield."*

# Contents

# Preface

Students of Southern intellectual history know Howard Washington Odum for his role in shaping and understanding the New South. His contributions to the modernization of the South are well documented by biographer Wayne Brazil, sociologist John Shelton Reed, historian George Tindall, student and colleague Rupert Vance, and historian Michael Milligan. Besides publishing over twenty-five books and more than one hundred articles of his own, among them his monumental work *Southern Regions of the United States* (1936), Odum founded and chaired the first department of sociology at the University of North Carolina at Chapel Hill.[1] At the university he created the Institute for Research in Social Science, founded the journal *Social Forces,* and oversaw University of North Carolina Press publications of a number of groundbreaking sociological studies of the South, among them works by Jesse Steiner and Roy Brown on prison chain gangs, Arthur Raper on lynchings, and Jennings Rhyne on mill workers.

Students of American musical history and folklore know Odum as one of the first collectors of African American blues and work songs, which he published in two volumes, *The Negro and His Songs* (1925) and *Negro Workaday Songs* (1926). Milligan and others conclude that Odum's central academic legacy "lies in the precious 'raw materials' of Negro folk life he was able to salvage" (20).

In the 1920s Odum and his student Guy B. Johnson saw the study of social relations, including race relations, as a key ingredient to practicing Christian good will toward their fellow human beings. However, the "good wishes" of these scholars did not preclude stereotyping

the subjects of their research. It would take two important friendships to change Odum's understanding of folklore and alter his racist
assumptions, one that developed from his evolving working relationship with Johnson, his younger, more liberal colleague, the other with
an extraordinary black informant, John Wesley "Left Wing" Gordon.
Although Odum was not originally trained as a folklorist, his interest
in African American music eventually led him to that discipline, and
he quickly grasped the collaborative and nonhierarchical nature of folk
studies. Ultimately, the study of African American folklore, based on
his collaborative work with Johnson and Gordon, changed Odum's
attitudes about race and culture.

A paragraph from the opening chapter of Odum and Johnson's
first collection of African American folk songs, *The Negro and His Songs,*
clearly illustrates the authors' well-meaning but essentially racist approach to their material:

> This volume may be said also to be an effort toward good will and good
> wishes. From this viewpoint the objective presentation has its advan-
> tages. If the musical nature and potential of the race can be emphasized
> again and again; if the good nature, the resourcefulness and adaptabil-
> ity of the Negro may be studied from varying viewpoints; if the Negro's
> skill and art may be presented in this way; if his hypocrisy and two-faced
> survival mechanisms may be suggested along with his good manners, his
> diplomacy, his artistic expression and rare harmony, then added values
> may be found in this volume. (9)

Like other Southern intellectuals of their day, Odum and Johnson
eventually became more tolerant in their racial views, and a chronological study of their folklore work provides clear documentation of
that process.

For folklorists, historians, and students of Southern literature, then,
Odum's folklore studies offer insights into the mind of a Southern white
intellectual, one seen by his contemporaries as a definite liberal but
who, in retrospect, seems quite conservative. Indeed, Odum's personal
and scholarly history clearly reveals a gradual but decided move from

racism to tolerance and, finally, to appreciation of African American folk culture's contributions to American culture. Although the scientific shift from heredity to environment as the determining factor in racial identity influenced Odum, the liberalizing of Odum's views on race occurred largely because he undertook folklore studies of African American culture. In other words, studying the folklore changed the folklorist.

This book explores some of the contributions that Odum, his colleagues, and his students made to the field of folklore studies, African American studies, and Southern intellectual history in the last century. Odum's work stands out as groundbreaking, in every sense of the term, in all three of these areas. His folklore and literary publications give us unique insights into the mind of a white Southern intellectual who lived during the first half of the twentieth century. My source materials are largely primary; they include Odum's letters and papers from the Southern Historical Collection and personal interviews with Odum's colleague Guy B. Johnson and his daughter, Mary Odum Schinhan.

Chapter 1, a biography, covers aspects of Odum's career that pertain to his folklore fieldwork. A number of other writers, including Wayne Brazil, Rupert Vance, and Daniel Singal, have written extensively about Odum's life as a sociologist. I examine Odum's career as a folklorist, including his formative early collecting in Mississippi and Georgia, his sociology dissertation, and his crucial collaborations with Guy Johnson and his chief African American informant, John Wesley Gordon.

Chapter 2 deals with Odum and Johnson's two folk-song collections, *The Negro and His Songs* and *Negro Workaday Songs*. Blues scholar David Evans criticizes the absence of musical notation in these books, declaring they are primarily useful because they contain some of the earliest written versions of a number of African American folk songs. Although I agree with Evans's assessment in part, I see additional value in Odum and Johnson's collections because the books provide important clues to understanding Odum's changing views on race. Collaborating with

Johnson on these collections also clearly altered Odum's views on the discipline of folklore as well.

Chapter 3 discusses Odum's three "folk" novels, the Black Ulysses trilogy, and analyzes Odum's fruitful collaboration with his primary informant, John Wesley Gordon. *Rainbow Round My Shoulder* is based on Gordon's travels around the South as an itinerant construction worker. *Wings on My Feet* follows his adventures in World War I. The third book, *Cold Blue Moon,* chronicles a series of ghost stories told by Gordon about the antebellum South. Examining Odum's literary theory in relation to these novels, as well as the authenticity of the African American folklore in the books, demonstrates Odum's changing approach to folklore studies.

Chapter 4 is a literary analysis of the three novels. In these works, Odum moves from a largely transcriptive use of folk material in the first novel to more functional uses of folklore in the later books. In addition, this chapter contains a close analysis of *Wings on My Feet,* the second Black Ulysses novel, arguably the best of the three from a literary standpoint. The chapter includes a discussion of Odum's narrative technique and a comparison of *Wings on My Feet*—a black man's memoir essentially ghostwritten by a white folklorist—to other World War I memoirs written by African American authors.

Daniel Singal believes that Odum wrote novels in order to distance himself from the painful truths of Southern racism. That view neglects the evidence that, as a result of his friendship with Gordon, Odum's attitudes on race had changed completely by the time he wrote his third novel. Thus, the distancing that Singal describes is Odum's attempt to make liberal racial views more palatable to his readers.

The fifth chapter describes Odum's contributions to American folklore and his literary legacy, including his influence on subsequent folklore research by Guy Johnson, the folk plays of Paul Green, and the publications of the University of North Carolina Press. Another part of his personal legacy is his family: both of Odum's sons became ecologists, an interesting continuation of his concern for the South, the land, and its people. Odum's personal and professional contributions as a folklore collaborator and mentor provide the focus for the concluding sixth chapter.

In many ways, this is a book about mentoring. Mentoring has a long tradition in American culture, going back to the apprentice system of the colonial era, which can be traced to European practices of the Middle Ages. In academics, we often focus on the hierarchy and fail to take advantage of the opportunities of reverse mentoring. Usually an older, experienced professor mentors a younger protégé, either student or colleague. Odum's early academic career followed this pattern; he was mentored by Thomas Pierce Bailey at the University of Mississippi and G. Stanley Hall at Clark University. When it was Odum's turn to mentor, however, he was less traditional, probably because of the nature of folklore studies. The discipline of folklore encourages collaboration and open-minded appreciation of other cultures. The field of folklore, by definition, is nonhierarchical and collaborative.

Students of folklore collect traditional material from folk artists, analyze it, and share it with the world. The artistic product clearly belongs to the artist; the folklorist may only claim to have "discovered" and studied the folk artist. But many early folklore scholars claimed the work of their informants as their own. To some extent, Odum belongs to this early group of researchers who did not carefully document their work. On the other hand, Odum's approach to the field of folklore—and his early racist assumptions about his informants—changed markedly over the course of his career, particularly from 1920 to 1935, when he was most active as a folklorist. These changes grew out of his mentor/mentee relationships.

Early on, Odum was willing to share authorship with mentee Guy Johnson; although Johnson was a graduate student when their two folksong collections were published, he is listed as coauthor, not second author. Likewise, Odum's fruitful collaboration with his chief African American informant, John Wesley Gordon, became less hierarchical as it developed. Although Odum, the established scholar, was the traditional "authority" in these relationships, he did not let this "natural order" define the roles of his collaborators. In many important ways, then, Johnson and Gordon were allowed to ignore the usual hierarchical relationship and become Odum's mentors. The results were profound: Johnson changed Odum's approach to the study of folklore; Gordon changed his views on race.

Eventually, Odum served as a folklore mentor to others, including North Carolina playwright Paul Green. Finally, of course, Odum served as academic mentor to his two sons, Howard T. Odum and Eugene Odum. His legacy as a folklorist is closely entwined with their work as ecologists. Howard Washington Odum's story, then, is the tale of how folk art and ordinary people, as well as arts, ideas, and intellectuals, can influence history.

# *Acknowledgments*

This book about mentoring, both traditional and collaborative, reflects my own academic career, which has benefited from both kinds. As an undergraduate at Appalachian State University, Thomas McGowan first introduced me to the field of folklore by agreeing to direct an independent study on Scottish customs during my semester of student teaching abroad. Since those early years, he has continued to support my career in numerous ways, by encouraging me to study folklore in graduate school and, once I became his colleague here at Appalachian State, inviting me to serve as his assistant editor on the *North Carolina Folklore Journal*. Tom is the most generous of colleagues and I am grateful for his many years of friendship.

Daniel Patterson, Kenan Professor Emeritus and former director of the curriculum in folklore at the University of North Carolina, suggested the folklore work of Howard Odum as a research topic and directed my dissertation with great insight and patience. His influence on my own teaching and scholarship has been profound, as it has been on the careers of many other folklorists.

Appalachian State University has been my academic home for much of my career; I am proud to be a member of an English department faculty that encourages collegiality and collaboration. A number of my colleagues have assisted me with this project. Cece Conway and Susan Staub offered advice and editing in the early stages of this work; Georgia Rhoades taught me about collaborative teaching and writing in actual practice; Mary Dunlap has supported my career for many years. I am especially grateful to Sandy Ballard and Grace McEntee, my writing group, who were so generous with their time, excellent editing skills, and friendship. Karen Baldwin, my folklore colleague at East Carolina University, offered important conceptual insights and advice.

Like Howard Odum, I have also benefited from reciprocal mentoring. My former student Ashley Nation Gaddy has often assisted me with my research, and her contributions to this project have been particularly helpful. However, her most important service has been caring for my three children, when they were young, and being a friend to our entire family. Now she is also pursuing a career in folklore.

I also appreciate the help of the librarians at the Southern Historical Collection and the North Carolina Collection at the University of North Carolina, and the guidance of the editing staff at the University of Georgia Press.

My most profound personal and academic mentoring came from my late father, Bill Moss. As a college professor himself, he was in the best position to advise and encourage me in my career. His unflagging faith in my abilities and seasoned perspective on the academic world, as well as his love, provided me with a model for the scholarly life. He would be amazed and proud of the ultimate results of his weekly calls many years ago, urging me to just "get that dissertation done."

My sister, Trudy Moss, a folklorist, media specialist, and advocate for multicultural education, also offered important insights and publishing advice for this book. A project that began as a dissertation many years ago evolved into a book after a number of conversations with my husband, Jim Sanders, about racial tolerance. I appreciate Jim's collaborative spirit in all aspects of our life together. I am grateful to him and to our incredible children, Laurel, Zeb, and Jordan, for their love and their support of all my endeavors.

Portions of this book were first published, in different form, in *Southern Cultures* 3, no. 2, and *Southern Literary Journal* 22, no. 1. Portions of chapter 5 © 1992 by *Southern Literary Journal* and the University of North Carolina at Chapel Hill Department of English. Reprinted by permission.

# Abbreviations

| | |
|---|---|
| CBM | *Cold Blue Moon (1931)* |
| NS | *The Negro and His Songs (1925)* |
| NWS | *Negro Workaday Songs (1926)* |
| RRMS | *Rainbow Round My Shoulder (1928)* |
| WOMF | *Wings on My Feet (1929)* |

CHAPTER ONE

# African American Folklore
# and Odum's Liberal Agenda
# at the University of North Carolina

W hen Harry Woodburn Chase was elected the tenth president of the University of North Carolina in June 1919, he laid out his plan for the institution in his first report to the university trustees. "My own conviction constantly deepens," he said, "that the next great creative chapter in the history of the nation is to be written here in the South. Here is now the real center of that pioneering spirit which has made America possible" (qtd. in Wilson 437–38). Chase felt, however, that industrial wealth and land were only two of North Carolina's resources; its most important resource was the young people of its schools and colleges. Chase saw that the South needed an institution of higher learning

> which typifies, and serves, and guides, this new civilization–an institution shot through with the spirit of service, broad and quick in its sympathies, practical in its training for the practical things of that life which in its astounding complexity confronts the new generation, insistent always that whatever is done shall be well done, stressing without cease the values that inhere in a liberal education so that its sons may know how to live as well as how to earn a living, resolutely keeping in the foreground those spiritual values by which alone a State can endure. My dream for the University of North Carolina is that she be nothing less than this. (qtd. in Wilson 438)

Part of Chase's dream was the establishment of a department of sociology at the University of North Carolina. His own training was in philosophy and the social sciences; he had studied under the well-known psychologist G. Stanley Hall at Clark University (Wilson 443). In 1920 Chase recommended that the university establish a chair of sociology and a school of public welfare. He believed that "if the citizenship of State and Nation is to grapple successfully with the ever more complex problems of modern democracy, if popular government is to work effectively in these confusing times, our educational system as a whole must stress as never before the instruction of our youth in matters of the common weal" (qtd. in Wilson 447).

While a graduate student at Clark University, Chase met Howard Washington Odum, and as a result of that meeting and their subsequent personal and professional friendship, Chase was determined to bring Odum to Chapel Hill. Odum, a native of Georgia, had received a B.A. from Emory College in 1904, an M.A. in classics from the University of Mississippi in 1906, a Ph.D. in psychology from Clark in 1909, and a second Ph.D. in sociology from Columbia University in 1910. At Columbia, Odum studied under Franklin H. Giddings, one of the leading sociologists in America. Odum had worked for the Philadelphia Bureau of Municipal Research from 1910 to 1912, taught at the University of Georgia from 1912 to 1919, and served as dean at Emory College from 1919 to 1920. He seemed ideally suited for the position Chase had in mind, and on February 27, 1920, Odum was named Kenan Professor of Sociology. In September 1920 the Department of Sociology and the School of Public Welfare opened, with Odum as chair.

Howard Washington Odum was a major force in the transition that the University of North Carolina made from a provincial local college to a nationally renowned university during the decades of the 1920s and 1930s. During his thirty-five-year tenure Odum helped to effect changes that still influence the state of North Carolina and the South today. His research, based on liberal ideals in politics, race relations, and religion, was the driving force for many of the intellectual changes in the South during the first half of the twentieth century.

In modern parlance, the meaning of the word "liberal" has become increasingly diffuse, ranging from a political label to an educational term. Historians studying the South during the early twentieth century generally connect the term "liberal" with race issues. Morton Sosna explains his use of the term:

> My test of the white Southern liberal lies in his stance on the race issue. I use the term broadly, classifying as "liberal" those white Southerners who perceived that there was a serious maladjustment of race relations in the South, who recognized that the existing system resulted in grave injustices for blacks, and who either actively endorsed or engaged in programs to aid Southern blacks in their fight against lynching, disfranchisement, segregation, and blatant discrimination in such areas as education, employment, and law enforcement. (*In Search of the Silent South* viii)

In his well-known study of race relations in the South, *The Crucible of Race* (1984), Joel Williamson defines a "liberal mentality" as one that was "relatively open-ended in its view of the future of the Negro in the nation; and, most essentially, it possessed a sanguine faith, an optimistic adventurousness, a willingness to experiment in a search for progress that other mentalities lacked" (5–6). Williamson notes that a number of early-twentieth-century Southern academics fit this description. He explains, "Many of these people were moved by paternalism, by a Southern Christian faith, and by a sensitivity that led to sympathy and action, but also many of them seemed to be moved most essentially by a fundamental rationalism—a sort of philosophical intellectualism that put great faith in research and reason while it damned irrationality and illogic" (489).

Williamson notes that often these academics became "liberal" because of their dedication to science and scholarship and the pursuit of truth. He also believes that sociologists and historians were especially likely to become liberals in the academy (489). Williamson goes on to point to Howard Odum as an example of a Southerner from a traditional background who took the path to liberalism, in part because of the influence of his teachers at Emory University (490).

Howard Odum was anxious to put his liberal agenda into action immediately upon his arrival in Chapel Hill. Although Odum spent a major portion of his first year at the University of North Carolina in getting the new Department of Sociology and School of Public Welfare underway, his interests and subsequent accomplishments soon expanded to areas such as race relations, the Southern mill town, politics, and agriculture. From 1920 until his retirement in 1954, Odum helped both President Harry Woodburn Chase and President Frank Porter Graham realize their goal of establishing the University of North Carolina as one of the leading universities in the country.

In addition to his personal achievements and his intellectual influence upon the university community, Odum helped create a modern research climate at the University of North Carolina, particularly with the publication of the *Journal of Social Forces,* begun in 1922, and the establishment of the Institute for Research in Social Science in 1924 (Wilson 449). Chase supported Odum's burgeoning research interests because he felt North Carolina's problems had been studied very little, especially "the characteristic mill village of the South . . . the race question . . . and the effects of the social and economic history of the region against which the whole development had to be viewed" (qtd. in Wilson 463).

Chase also felt that the people's idea of the function of government had changed; government was now seen as an agency for promoting the welfare of the state and its people. Therefore he supported Odum's establishment of the institute for the purpose of "the cooperative study of problems in the general field of social science arising out of state and regional conditions" (qtd. in Wilson 463). Through the work of the institute, Odum and his colleagues were able to contribute to the development of the state and its efficiency in serving the people.

The Institute for Research in Social Science opened in September 1924, and in 1927 Odum was named director. Other staff members included Guy B. Johnson, Harriet Herring, Roy M. Brown, and H. D. Meyer. According to Louis R. Wilson, a member of the Board of Governors, "The impact of the Institute upon North Carolina and the South was electric. It immediately brought the social and economic problems of the State and region under careful survey, and through its publications, it greatly extended interest in and understanding of State and Southern social problems" (Wilson 467). The institute also supported the graduate school by providing research assistantships, and it "cut across departmental lines and concentrated the thinking of a large group of faculty members upon the social and economic development of the region" (467). The institute funded the research for such diverse projects as Harriet Herring's work on the mill village, Roy M. Brown's research on prison chain gangs, and H. D. Meyer's research on recreation.

According to Louis Wilson, the Institute for Research in Social Science also helped support the newly established University of North Carolina Press, founded in 1922, for "it not only supplied manuscripts for publication but financial assistance in establishing its growing reputation as a regional publishing medium" (Wilson 468). The UNC Press published Odum and Johnson's two folk-song collections, *The Negro and His Songs* (1925) and *Negro Workaday Songs* (1927); Johnson's book *John Henry* (1929) and his *Folk Culture on St. Helena Island* (1930); Odum's *Southern Regions of the United States* (1936); and other works by these two men, their colleagues, and their students. In 1924 the UNC Press adopted a motion by Odum to accept manuscripts from all over the country, thus ensuring the growth of a national reputation (Wilson 492).

The organization and subsequent expansion of the University of North Carolina Press was another aspect of the growth of UNC into a modern university. Wilson concludes that the spirit of the times greatly influenced the establishment of the press. The university "clearly conceived its role as that of a great organic institution created and supported by the State as its principal agency for training the experts who were to serve it in all aspects of its expanding life" (Wilson 487–88). Just as the presses at Oxford, Cambridge, Harvard, and Yale had "demonstrated the importance of publication as a function of the modern university," so the establishment of the UNC Press was a major step in bringing North Carolina's university system into step with the twentieth century (Wilson 488).

Howard Odum was not only instrumental in developing these institutions at the University of North Carolina, but he also achieved a great deal professionally as well. When he retired in June 1954, Odum had been awarded honorary L.L.D.s from Emory (1931) and Harvard (1939), and an L.H.D. from Clark (1941). He had also served as president of the American Sociological Society (1930), associate editor of *Recent Social Trends in the U.S.* (1931), founder of *Social Forces* (1922), and had published numerous articles and books, including the monumental *Southern Regions of the United States* (1936).

## Regionalism and the New South Movement

Howard Washington Odum is remembered today for his practical contributions to the University of North Carolina, the state, and the region. Odum's best-known contribution to sociology is *Southern Regions of the United States* (1936), a nearly seven-hundred-page compilation and analysis of various aspects of Southern culture, including agriculture, industry, technology, and folkways. In the introduction, Odum expresses the hope that the work would serve as a "relatively comprehensive and enduring index of regional culture which may be variously utilized; as a basis for practical planning and specialized research; as a basis for later comparative studies of the same regions; as a basis for comparative studies of other regions; as hypothetical basis for subsequent regional and subregional classification and analysis; as an introduction to the appraisal of American regional cultures" (x).

Odum believed that cataloging the traits of the South was the first step toward merging the region with the rest of the nation while maintaining its distinctive culture. Most sociologists and Southern historians cite Odum's work in *Southern Regions* as his primary published contribution to the field of Southern studies. Odum's obituary in the *Washington Post* on November 14, 1954, described him as "the Eli Whitney of the modern South," saying he "inspired a revolution. . . . It has been said that his *Southern Regions of the United States* . . . did as much to arouse the South economically as *Uncle Tom's Cabin* did to arouse the North sociologically before the Civil War" (Odum Papers).

Recent historians have noted that Odum's theoretical contributions to the intellectual milieu of the South are perhaps his most important legacy. As historian George Tindall explains, Odum's theory of "new regionalism" ultimately had a theoretical rather than a practical influence on Southern liberal thought ("Significance" 305). The term "regionalism" in literary criticism usually describes literature written about a certain region; Odum's "new regionalism," however, was a sociological theory emphasizing the need for a progressive South that would become united with the rest of the nation without losing its regional culture.

Odum's plan was national in scope; he repudiated the current trend of sectionalism or localism, which affirmed cultural differences in America, in favor of a regionalism that could unify Americans in order to solve common problems while still maintaining the cultural diversity that was the root of society, the "universal societal constant in a world of historical variable" (*Folk, Region, and Society* 219). He explained that "the primary objectives of regionalism are found in the end product of integration of regions more than the mere study and development of regions themselves" (199).

In an unpublished "Work Memorandum" written in March 1947, Odum clarified his theory:

> *Regionalism* is essentially the framework for the scientific study of regional cultures in relation to the total or composite society of which they are constituent parts. All cultures have their genesis and grow up in the physical regional setting, expand in multitudes of a varied social structure, and retain a perspective to their component regional conditioning. Regionalism, therefore, is a key to folk-sociology which also studies *comparative society* through regional folk culture. (18)

*Southern Regions* was hailed as a monumental work by many, but it was not without its critics, particularly Donald Davidson and other members of the Agrarian group at Vanderbilt, whose plan for the South's future had been published in a collection of essays entitled *I'll Take My Stand* (1930). The Agrarians felt the traditional rural life of the South offered more hope for the future of the region than what seemed to be the blind dedication of many Southern liberals to following the North's precedent of industrial development (xix). The Agrarians saw regionalism, because of its progressive overtones, as a theory that could do away with the South's greatest virtue, its rural folk culture. Donald Davidson voiced this criticism of regionalism in his book *The Attack on Leviathan: Regionalism and Nationalism in the United States* (1938), which, interestingly, was published by the UNC Press.

Modern critics of the Agrarians' philosophy conclude that they were merely unwilling to accept necessary change, and that their reluctance stemmed both from a racist philosophy and from an idealized picture of Southern folk culture. In fact, the Agrarian philosophy enjoyed some popularity, but as Louis Rubin Jr. writes in his introduction to a modern edition of *I'll Take My Stand*, "The South and the nation cannot be said to have heeded its economic, political and social counsels to any startling effect. The industrialization of the South proceeded apace" (ix). On the other hand, as Morton Sosna writes in his analysis of Southern racial liberalism, *In Search of the Silent South,* Odum's regionalism "became the widely accepted Southern liberal alternative to the steadfast, sometimes Negrophobic agrarianism of a heretic faction of white liberals, the Vanderbilt 'fugitives'" (55).

Regionalism was not only an important influence on social theory in the South; it influenced Southern writers as well. Odum's folklore and sociological research provided a statistical basis for the need for social reform in the South, the theme of many of the writers of the Southern Renaissance. His work also paralleled that of local writers of the time, particularly writers involved in the Carolina Folk Play movement. In fact, Odum served as something of a mentor to one of the Carolina Playmakers, Paul Green.

Clearly, Chase's invitation to Odum was a turning point in his career. The University of North Carolina was an environment conducive for Odum to begin synthesizing his theory of regionalism with his interest in race relations. His own subsequent invitation to Guy Johnson to live in Chapel Hill helped forge the relationships that were to completely change his approach to sociology.

## Odum's Academic Background

Howard Odum's background is one reason he ultimately disagreed with the Nashville Agrarians about the best plan for the future of the South. Unlike some of the Fugitive group, whose ideas of the folk were idealized and literary, Odum had first-hand experience with the best and the worst of rural Southern life. As with other turn-of-the-century Southern liberals, Odum's ideas on culture and race were formed by a synthesis of his religious background and his education.

Howard Washington Odum was born in Bethlehem, Georgia, in 1884. Odum's father was a farmer; his mother's father was a successful antebellum plantation owner. Odum's mother had been forced to marry beneath her social class because the Civil War had devastated her family's fortunes, and she encouraged Howard's education in the belief that it would help him regain the social status she had lost. Both of Odum's parents were deeply religious Protestants. His father put his Christianity to active use and worked for the improvement of the lot of his neighbors, especially in the area of agricultural reform (Brazil 1, 8, 11, 114).

Odum worked on the family farm when he was young, and he attended school in Oxford, Georgia. He began to realize his mother's ambitions for his future when he received a bachelor's degree in classics from Emory College in 1904. In *The Crucible of Race,* Joel Williamson describes Odum's experience as a student of Andrew Sledd, a Latinist who was "reputedly partial to that early egalitarian Cicero." Odum studied with Sledd during 1901–2. Later, Sledd was forced to leave Emory for "having written in the *Atlantic Monthly* that, among other things, lynching was a crime" (490).

The best job Odum could find upon graduation was as a schoolteacher in Tocopolla, Mississippi; he taught there briefly before pursuing a master's degree in classics at the University of Mississippi. Odum's experiences in Mississippi profoundly influenced the course of his future career, especially his attitudes toward race, the social sciences, and folklore. Odum's psychology professor, Thomas Pierce

Bailey, had studied with the pioneering psychologist G. Stanley Hall at Clark University and arranged for Odum to attend graduate school there. Hall, a hereditarian, believed human moral and psychological development paralleled the evolutionary development of the race: those who are unable to progress beyond the savage state must obey those who are more advanced. Bailey applied Hall's theories of character formation to the "Negro Problem" in the South, and, although he was concerned about the status of Southern blacks, he, like many Southern white "liberals" at that time, assumed that African Americans were intellectually and morally inferior to whites. Wayne Brazil, Odum's biographer, speculates that Odum changed his academic focus from the classics to the social sciences as a result of Bailey's influence and the legacy of "the commitment to social service that his parents had embraced as an essential part of their religion" (114–15). Odum's subsequent graduate work was based on this same idea of practical Christianity combined with a scientific approach to studying the people of another culture.

While he lived in Mississippi, Odum began collecting African American folk songs in churches and communities, and these songs formed the basis of his 1909 doctoral dissertation in psychology from Clark University. Although studies of American folklorists reveal that Odum was certainly not alone in his interest in African American folk music, his social science perspective on the material was novel.

Shortly after completing his dissertation for his degree in psychology, Odum published much of the folk-song material in three articles; he separated the sections on religious song and secular song for publication. "Religious Folk-Songs of Southern Negroes" was published in the *American Journal of Religious Psychology and Education* (July 1909). That a journal of "religious psychology and education" even existed early in the twentieth century is testament to the substantial changes that have occurred in the social science disciplines since Odum obtained a Ph.D. in psychology. The editors' interest in Odum's work as a valuable contribution to understanding the "psychology" of African Americans underscores the fact that Odum was not alone in his racist assumptions about folk material. Odum recognized the originality of his work on secular song, however, and published two articles on "Folk-Song and Folk-Poetry: As Found in the Secular Songs of the Southern Negroes" in the *Journal of American Folklore* (1911). Thus, the publication of a portion of his psychology dissertation represents Odum's inaugural work as a folklorist.

Odum's early folk-song collections are unique in their focus on the social and psychological aspects of African American folk song. In his article "Religious Folk-Songs" Odum writes, "Posterity has often judged peoples without having so much as a passing knowledge of their inner life" (1–2). He explains that the study of folklore is important not only because it is a historical science but because of its "essential value in the study of psychological, anthropological, and sociological conditions" (2). Odum theorized that a study of folk music could lead to greater insights into a culture, and he approached his subject by an unusual method that combined the disciplines of art and social science in order to achieve a window on his informants' "inner lives."

In his dissertation, Odum ignored the demographic data on race that are usually the basis of any study of culture. Instead, he concentrated on the artistic products of the culture, something other folklorists had done but without a sociological intent; for example, Cecil Sharp collected Appalachian folk songs, but not with the professed purpose of seeing into the "heart and soul" of a race and thus improving race relations. Sharp had some interest in proving that the mountaineer was not ignorant though he might be illiterate and that his culture was of a longstanding and honorable tradition, but Sharp did not present the songs in an effort to affect the mountaineer's social condition.

Although Odum's article mentions the "natural poetic spirit and the power of the imagination" found in these songs, he was not primarily interested in their literary qualities. Odum collected the songs because he believed they represented "the best conception of his [the African American's] religious, moral, mental and social tendencies" (4); thus the songs offer an expressive and concrete, if not statistical, method of studying African American culture. Odum found the study of religious folk song important, he explained, because "In no way can a better insight into the negro's religion be obtained than by a careful study of his songs" (23). Today, despite his best intentions, these so-called insights often seem preconceived, serving to support ready-made notions and stereotypes about the black "character."

Both Odum's "good works" approach to sociology and his essentially racist assumptions are apparent in his 1910 doctoral dissertation in sociology from Columbia University, subsequently published under the title *Social and Mental Traits of the Negro* (1910). Although he claimed "it would be a serious mistake to assume that all Negroes are alike in character and conduct" (16), he continually referred to "the Negro" as one group with universal traits and approached the "Negro Problem" as a racial problem. In reading the various chapters–"Negro Schools," "The Negro Church," "The Home Life"–it is obvious that Odum had interviewed individual African Americans, but as a sociologist, he felt compelled to generalize his findings as applying to an entire ethnic group. Thus, he made racist statements, describing "the onrush of his [the African American's] animal nature which leads him to neglect and abuse himself, his home and his family" and "the frequent instances in which the weakness of the black race is accorded patience by the stronger race" (14). He referred to blacks as "by nature and cultivation secretive" (18). Because Odum was trained as a sociologist to study groups, he lapsed into generalizations; it is easier to stereotype groups of people than individuals. Only much later in his life would a friendship with an individual black man temper Odum's racist ideas.

## Odum and the "Folk"

An understanding of Odum's definition of the term *folk* is the first step toward assessing his folklore studies. Rupert B. Vance, one of Odum's students and later a colleague at the University of North Carolina, discusses Odum's concept of "the folk" in an unpublished paper entitled "Howard W. Odum and the Case of the South." Vance says that Odum's thinking on the subject of "the folk" was based on his reading of such works as Wilhelm Wundt's *Folk Psychology* (translated 1916) and William Graham Sumner's *Folkways: A Study of the Sociological Importance of Usages, Manners, Customs, Mores, and Morals* (1907). According to Vance, Odum "asserted that when old civilizations such as those of Greece and Rome passed away," new cultures arose "from the folk." But Odum did not idealize the folk. Vance says Odum "regarded Hitlerism, which he abhorred, as basically a folk movement. His primary concern was to understand the process of change from folk culture to mature state-civilization, from a society characterized by folkways to a transitional one, characterized by technicways, and finally, to one in which stateways predominate" (n.p.).

George L. Simpson, also one of Odum's students and colleagues, writes in "Howard W. Odum and American Regionalism" that to Odum the folk represented "that elemental universal process of human association wherein the individual, the family, kinship, the community, informal controls, realistic relation to nature, and significant reference to the past and its cultural conditioning constitute the basic, surviving mode of life" (102–3).

In an article in *The Folklore Historian*, Michael J. Milligan explains that Odum differed from early anthropologists in his willingness to apply "lessons of past cultures" to the "present cultural crisis" (15).

Odum's own discussion of the folk appears in an unpublished work memorandum entitled "On Trying to Define the Field and Methods of a Dynamic Folk Sociology" (written March 1947). "In the folk," he writes, "nearer than anything else, may be found the common denominator of the societal process" (1). The term *folk* does not "necessarily denote the primitive or preliterate," nor is it synonymous with the term "people" (10, 11). He goes on to say, "The term *folk,* then, designates process and product of interaction between and among people and between people and their environment on the level of primary institutions and spontaneous and homogeneous ideologies. The folk process persists in all societies" (12). Odum's emphasis here on *process,* or performance, is very modern; most folklorists of the time concentrated on the *product,* or text.

Odum's folklore studies, his sociological research, and his theory of regionalism are all based on his belief that folk societies can be a part of urban civilizations without detriment to either, and for him, the question of the future is whether "the society of the United States, for instance, is or will be folk society or state civilization, or the happy blending of the two" (13). The solution is balance and equilibrium in three areas: "Regional balance and equality of man," balance "between the folk culture and the state civilization," and "balance between individuation and socialization" (18). Odum felt that folklore studies were the first step in achieving this balance because the roots of a culture must be understood before it could be changed for the better.

Odum had formulated his rationale for folklore studies as early as 1909, when he opened his article "Religious Folk-Songs" as follows:

> To know the soul of a people and to find the source from which flows the expression of folk-thought is to comprehend in a large measure the capabilities of that people. To obtain the truest expression of the folk-mind and feeling is to reveal much of the inner-consciousness of the race. . . .
> In the study of race character the value of true expressions of the feelings and mental imagery cannot be overestimated. . . . To bring a people face to face with themselves and to place them fairly before the world is the first service that can be rendered in the solution of race problems. (1)

"As a part of folklore," folk music adds to our understanding of culture because "it represents less of the traditional and more of the spontaneous" (2). Folk songs are especially important in the study of African American culture since "In revealing much of what he *is* rather than what he *appears to be,* the folk-songs of the Southern negro are superior to any superficial study made from partial observations. The insight into negro character gained from their folk-songs and poetry accompanied by careful and exhaustive concrete social studies may be accepted as impartial testimony" (3). Odum also suggests that if African American religious songs are to be preserved, they need to be collected now, before they disappear altogether in the face of progress.

Odum's thesis that a study of folk music can lead to greater insights into a culture is interesting from both a sociological and folkloric standpoint. As Tindall explains, Odum is combining two disciplines, social science and art, an unusual method at the time but one that anticipates some modern studies of culture. For example, in *The Anthropology of Music* (1964), Alan P. Merriam explains that his field, ethnomusicology, attempts to unite the social sciences and humanities. Ethnomusicologists, who study "a product of the humanistic side of man's existence . . . must at the same time realize that the product is the result of behavior which is shaped by the society and culture of the men who produce it" (25). According to Merriam, music is particularly adaptable to a research method that combines science with art because it is "a uniquely human phenomenon which exists only in terms of social interaction; that is, it is made by people for other people, and it is learned behavior" (27).

Thus, Odum from the start was clearly on the cutting edge of his discipline. He combined his early interest in classical civilizations, his own background as a Southern white, and his interest in social science and social reform into a comprehensive theory of folklore, one that took the new approach of viewing artistic products of a culture from a scientific viewpoint. Although he did not put these ideas on paper until 1947, they obviously influenced the kinds of studies he undertook early in his career. His folklore research is based on the belief that through scientific study folk culture can be both preserved and successfully merged with state civilization. It is a tribute to Odum's thought and influence that this view of progress is still influential in the South today.

## Folklore as an Emerging Discipline

Howard Odum was one of a number of "accidental" or untrained folklorists who made significant contributions to the field during the early twentieth century. Some of these collectors were not academics at all; others, like Odum, were highly trained specialists from other fields whose interests and expertise were well suited to interdisciplinary studies.

The most famous of these collectors, of course, is Harvard professor Francis James Child, a Chaucer scholar who collected and edited *The English and Scottish Popular Ballads* (5 vols., 1882–98). The British scholar Cecil J. Sharp (1859–1924), with the help of his former student Maud Karpeles (1886–1976), collected ballads in the Appalachian mountains, and published *English Folk Songs from the Southern Appalachians* in 1917. The UNC Press published *Folk Beliefs of the Southern Negro* (1926) by sociology professor Newbell Niles Puckett of Western Reserve University in Cleveland. Dorothy Scarborough, a novelist and teacher of creative writing at Columbia University, published *On the Trail of Negro Folksongs* in 1925 and *A Song Catcher in the Southern Mountains* in 1937.

In her chapter "The Literary Folklorists" in *American Folklore Scholarship: A Dialogue of Dissent* (1988), Rosemary Zumwalt describes the humanities background and focus of these and other early-twentieth-century folklore scholars. Archer Taylor, well-known collector of riddles and proverbs, began his academic career as a German teacher (53–54). Ralph Steele Boggs, who founded the folklore curriculum at the University of North Carolina, was an English professor (54). Stith Thompson, another English professor who began his studies at Harvard, eventually collected North American Indian tales and published two of the folklorist's most useful tools, *The Types of the Folk-tale, A Classification and Bibliography* (1928), translated and enlarged from Antti Aarne's *Verzeichnis der Märchentypen*, and the *Motif-Index of Folk-Literature* (6 vols., 1932–36). Zumwalt explains that one of the aims of both anthropologists and literary folklorists associated with the American Folklore Society was the preservation of material that might otherwise be lost. She concludes that folklore scholars with humanities backgrounds focused on texts and their genres and defined the folk as members of the peasant culture (99–100).

Zumwalt and other folklore historians note the dominance of the anthropological folklorists in the American Folklore Society and its publications during the early part of the twentieth century. The most influential anthropologist of the early twentieth century, Franz Boas (1858–1942), was primarily interested in the folklore of American Indians because it represented a "type of cultural autobiography" (*American Folklore Encyclopedia* 20). According to folklore scholar W. K. McNeil, Boas's "belief in a superorganic concept of culture made any interest in those who preserve and pass on folklore irrelevant; the recording of texts was all that one needed" (20).

Even among the anthropologists there were untrained scholars who contributed to the field. Boas encouraged his secretary and editorial assistant, Ruth Bunzel, to pursue her interest in Native American artists; she went on to publish an important study, *The Pueblo Potter,* in 1929 (Zumwalt 74). According to Zumwalt, Boas, his students, and other early anthropological folklorists focused on culture rather than texts in their studies (99). Also, for the anthropologists, "the folk were members of non-Western, tribal cultures" (100). Both literary and anthropological folklorists, however, agreed on the necessity of studying one American folk group, African Americans, although "the literary folklorist emphasized the European elements and the anthropological folklorist emphasized the African" in the focus of their work (100).

The earliest collection of African American folk song is found in *Slave Songs of the United States* (1867), a joint effort by William Francis Allen, Charles Pickard Ware, Lucy McKim Garrison, and various other collectors. The writers of this book were not "folklorists, anthropologists, or musicologists" but missionaries to the Sea Islands during the Civil War who were sympathetic to the slaves' cause (Wilgus 347). Allen explains the hope of the editors that the religious and secular songs in the collection "should not be forgotten or lost, but that these relics of a state of society which has passed away should be preserved while it is still possible" (iii). In their studies of African American folk song, Odum and Johnson continued the work of these early scholars and added new material and insights to folk-song scholarship.[1]

Eventually, folklore studies became less of a hobby for either amateurs or scholars as it acquired the status of an academic field of inquiry. In his discussion of the history of the American Folklore Society, Simon J. Bronner explains that early in the twentieth century "a line of professional folklore interest already existed among philologists, medieval and classical scholars, and scholars of literature and languages" who "tended to have places in the university." "Literary interest in folklore ran high," according to Bronner, but "as a result of the American Folklore Society's original 'scientific,' professional orientation outside of academia and popular literature, the anthropological current gained strength" (16). Bronner also speculates that the "upsurge in studies of American literature and arts in the 1920s," as a result of modernism, increased the intellectual interest in folklore studies and American studies (98). While the field of anthropology was transformed by the reorganization of American universities into departments during the early twentieth century, folklore was not given "a departmental foothold." "To arise separately," Bronner continues, "folklore studies had to come from a coalition and a transformation of departmental forces. That occurred with a coalition of language, literature, and music interests that helped forge the early folklore curricula at Indiana, North Carolina, and Pennsylvania universities" (97).

Although Odum published portions of his folk-song dissertation in the *Journal of American Folklore,* he did not claim to be a folklorist. As a sociologist, he was largely unconcerned with the politics of the American Folklore Society and the struggle for power between the literary scholars and anthropologists whom Zumwalt discusses in her history of folklore studies. Odum also differed from some of the armchair folklorists of his day in that he did not see himself as primarily a collector. Allen, Child, and Sharp hoped to collect folk songs and ballads in America before they were lost entirely to popular culture; Puckett and Scarborough collected African American folklore as examples of a more "primitive" culture. Odum, like Boas, viewed folklore as "cultural autobiography," but his purposes for collecting set him apart from both the literary and anthropological folklore scholars and collectors of his day. When Odum wrote that the purpose of folklore was "to bring a people face to face with themselves and to place them fairly before the world" as a "service that can be rendered in the solution of race problems" ("Religious Folk-Songs" 1), he was confronting political and ethical issues that are still a matter of debate among folklorists and anthropologists today.

## Odum and the South of the 1920s

To understand the pioneering nature of Odum's research and fieldwork in the area of black music, we must first understand both the social and political context in which he was working. In 1926 Edwin Mims, Southerner and contemporary of Odum, wrote in *The Advancing South:* "It makes no difference how far the South may go in its progress toward liberalism, or how optimistic one may become over the outcome of the struggle with the forces of reaction, there is the everlasting race problem to shake the confidence in the future" (257). Mims characterizes the typical conservative Southerner as one who is still dominated by the idea of racial separation, who sees no future for African Americans, and who, "defeated in a long war and inheriting the provincialism and sensitiveness of a feudal order . . . remained proud in his isolation" (3). Coupled with these attitudes was Southerners' fear of criticism, from either Northerners or enlightened Southerners, which further isolated them from the influence of new ideas.

Odum understood these conservative Southerners and their reaction to liberalism because he had lived much of his early life in Georgia and Mississippi, where conservatism was strong. However, his home state, Georgia, was also the home of the New South movement, "first found in a group of far-seeing, liberal-minded Georgians" and particularly supported by Henry Grady, editor of the *Atlanta Constitution.* After 1876 Grady was "an exponent of the idea that the future of the South lay primarily not in politics, but in an industrial order which should be the basis of a more enduring civilization" (Mims 7). Other Georgia liberals were Atticus G. Haywood, president of Emory College and author of *Our Brother in Black,* and J. L. M. Curry, leader of the movement for the development of a public school system in Georgia and the South. But

Georgia failed to fulfill the promise of its leaders, as did other Southern states, according to Mims. He writes, "The stage seems all set for wonderful progress; the obstacles seem to be removed; and then something happens; there is a resurgence of the old, reactionary spirit, policies, and ideas." So the "sceptre of Southern leadership passed to North Carolina" (9).

The promise of Georgia had also failed for Odum. While serving as dean of the School of Liberal Arts at Emory University in Atlanta, he found it difficult to work with Bishop Warren A. Candler and the "ultraconservative Methodist power structure that controlled the school" (Johnson, *Research* 11). He was ready to move on, and the offer of a position at the University of North Carolina seemed the perfect opportunity.

One of the reasons liberal leadership flowered in North Carolina was the presence of a strong democratic spirit in the state. Although not blind to reactionary thought, Odum did see signs of greater liberalism in North Carolina than elsewhere in the South. He writes of this liberalism and democratic spirit in a letter to Will Alexander of the Inter-Racial Commission:

> There is one characteristic in many of the communities here which is
> of interest. I might illustrate this way: The University of North Carolina
> has done more extension and social work perhaps than any other univer-
> sity, and yet until one year ago it had no Department of Sociology. . . .
> There seems to be a most progrssive [*sic*] and wholesome spirit of coop-
> eration with the negroes in North Carolina. (July 19, 1921)

In this letter, Odum goes on to describe the essential paradox of Southern race relations, a general spirit of cooperation along with renewed interest in the Ku Klux Klan. Political and religious liberalism also had mixed support in North Carolina. But if individuals and groups were not always open-minded, the leadership at the University of North Carolina was clear in its support of liberal thought and action. According to Mims, none of the scholars at Chapel Hill could have done their work "if they had not had the cooperation of a wise and courageous president." Mims is of course speaking of Harry Woodburn Chase, a man who believes "there is a very definite need of facilities for investigation . . . in the whole field of what might be called human relationships. . . . And that is why he has backed to the limit the work done by Professors Odum and Branson in the field of sociology" (135, 137).

Odum had great admiration for Chase and his plans for the expansion of the university. In a letter to Albert Bushnell Hart, Odum expresses this admiration. He writes that Chase

> is an exponent of genuine democracy as expressed by the best ideals
> of political science, as I understand it. . . . While he is a native of Massa-
> chusetts, it seems to me as I talked with him in private life and watched
> his public work that he is in spirit a Southerner of Southerners, in so far
> as his love and ambition for the South go. (March 20, 1920)

Odum also felt challenged by Chase's plan for the future, particularly in regard to his own new duties as director of the School of Public Welfare. In the same letter to Hart, Odum calls the new school "one of the most distinctive steps in newer university administration." He goes on to explain that

> North Carolina has very advanced social legislation and the University is
> fitting into the State Program with commendable service and dispatch.
> There is every indication that such cooperation will be given the Uni-
> versity by certain other agencies, that it will have a real school of social
> work for the South next year with adequate professional standards, as
> well as emphasizing government and other social sciences in the regular
> curriculum, the doing of "social engineering work" throughout the State,
> and the promoting of greater research.

Mims agrees with Odum's assessment of the influence of the state university on North Carolina. "If North Carolina has one of the most enlightened departments of Social Welfare now existing," he writes, "it is largely due to the cooperation of the departments of Sociology and Rural Economics" at the University of North Carolina (118).

When Odum arrived in Chapel Hill in 1920, he had great plans and pretty clear ideas about how to accomplish his goals. He was also quite aware of the possible political implications of his future work and tried to achieve in advance a compromise between progress and radicalism. His close relationship with Chase aided his efforts to do so. In a letter to Chase dated May 3, 1920, three months before Odum's new position actually began, he wrote:

> I sometimes feel the humor of the situation in which I find myself: If I go too fast in this matter, your honorable faculty proclaim that here is a presumptious [sic] fellow who believes that his school is the whole show. If on the other hand, I wait until my tenure of office begins and let the big things slip by, "behold," they say, "see how this man doth not make good nor deliver thereunto the goods." You, of course, know what I mean and will be able to disseminate any opinion needed for the good of the work.

Odum's political sensitivity is evident in his choice of African American music as the first topic for investigation by the newly founded Institute for Research in Social Science. Guy Johnson, Odum's research assistant and later colleague and coauthor, said Odum wanted the institute's first project to be something quick and noncontroversial. Johnson paraphrased Odum's rationale: "I think if we just went in for studying race relations, which is your main interest I know, nobody's going to pay much attention and we might get in a lot of trouble because things are so conservative. But practically everybody, no matter how narrow-minded he is will say, 'Oh the Negro is a natural musician, he's a great singer,' and even conservative people can appreciate black music, so here we've got this chance, so let's do this" (interview 1985).

Odum not only wanted a noncontroversial topic, he wanted a quick publication from the institute, another reason for choosing to write on African American music. Odum had been interested in black culture since the early 1900s, even before he wrote his dissertation on folk song. When he studied at the University of Mississippi he often visited black churches and families on Sundays and copied down the texts of the songs they sang. "He must have had a whole trunkful of notes, not only on songs, but on customs, riddles, sayings, and so forth," says Johnson, only some of which had been published in his dissertation (interview). So Guy Johnson's first job as research assistant at the IRSS was to sort through Odum's trunkful of notes and make a book out of them. Odum may have been motivated by his ambitions for the institute, but the greatest rewards he reaped were personal: working with Johnson became the first significant experience in altering Odum's perception of "the Negro."

CHAPTER TWO

# Odum and Johnson's Collaborative Folk-Song Collections

F olklorists are more interested in people than books or texts. Howard Odum eventually became a consummate folk-lorist, in part because his interest in people led him to collaborators with less obvious "status." Odum was not too hierarchical to be influenced by both his student Guy Johnson and, later, his working-class African American informant, John Wesley Gordon. By the mid-1920s Odum had published only a portion of the trunkful of songs he had collected in Mississippi and Georgia in 1905 and later. He had completed the important early fieldwork; now he needed help turning both his previously published and unpublished texts into folk-song collections.

Odum's choice of Guy Benton Johnson as his first research assistant at the University of North Carolina was fortuitous. They struck up a letter-writing acquaintance through a mutual friend, Wiley Sanders, who had roomed with Johnson while they attended the graduate program in sociology at the University of Chicago. After returning to his home state, Texas, Johnson married Guion Griffis, and they both taught at Baylor College for Women. Johnson published several articles in *Social Forces* and was persuaded by Odum to pursue his doctorate at the University of North Carolina. The Johnsons moved to Chapel Hill in 1924 and both began graduate work, Guy in sociology and Guion in social history. The UNC Press published her dissertation, *Ante-Bellum North Carolina: A Social History,* in 1937. Guy Johnson's own work was sidetracked by the books he and Odum coauthored, but he completed a sociology dissertation, "A Study of the Musical Talent of the American Negro," in 1927. The Johnsons were associated with the Institute for Research in Social Science for many years and in 1980 coauthored a history of the Institute entitled *Research in Service to Society.*

Guy Johnson brought three important skills to Odum's work: editorial expertise, more up-to-date sociological training, and a musical gift. His contributions to Odum's work were largely editorial, but he also helped Odum broaden his definition of "folk" and his understanding of African American culture.

First, Johnson had a knack for turning Odum's long, semi-poetic phrases into clear and interesting prose. Johnson explained that Odum "had these long, meandering sentences . . . trying to cover the whole world, and sometimes he just had a hard time trying to see whether or not this actually made a grammatical sentence, because he might have a set of dashes or parentheses and this thing would go on half a page" (interview 1985). Although critics would continue to comment on the defects of Odum's prose style, Johnson did much to make it readable. The combination of Odum's research and Johnson's editing proved successful. The two published their first book, *The Negro and His Songs,* in 1925, one year after Johnson's arrival in Chapel Hill. *Negro Workaday Songs* followed a year later.

Johnson's second important contribution to Odum's work was the training in sociology he acquired at the University of Chicago. The study of sociology had progressed a great deal since Odum finished his work at Columbia in 1910, and by the 1920s the University of Chicago was on the cutting edge of research in the field. In *The Chicago School of Sociology* (1984), Martin Bulmer explains that in the 1920s "the earlier marriage of fact-finding with moralism—characteristic of the social survey movement—was replaced by a more mature view of the relation between social science and social action" (8). An emphasis on objective social science, without moralizing, characterizes Johnson's own research and clearly influenced the joint work he did with Odum. In *The War Within,* Daniel Singal concludes that Johnson was a "cultural anthropologist in all but name," and he credits Johnson with being the "student leading the teacher" in modifying Odum's segregationist racial views, particularly because the environmentalists were winning against the hereditarians in the philosophical discussions on racial characteristics (143).

Finally, Johnson's interest in music—he was an accomplished pianist—helped broaden the scope of the two folk-song collections he and Odum published. His musical knowledge was an especially important influence on the second book because he was able to persuade Odum that the addition of tunes to texts was essential.

Although Johnson made important contributions to folk-music studies and ultimately had a profound influence on Odum's racial views, the original fieldwork for their joint projects was Odum's. Howard Odum was one of the very earliest collectors of black folk music, beginning with his fieldwork in Mississippi and Georgia from 1905 through 1908. The songs he collected there were first published in his psychology dissertation and then in three articles, one in the *American Journal of Religious Psychology and Education,* two others in the *Journal of American Folklore.*

## Odum's Folk-Song Dissertation and Articles

Odum's early research in the field of black folk music was first published in his 1909 dissertation for a Ph.D. in psychology from Clark University. That the study of African American folk music was seen as appropriate material for a psychology study indicates how desperate white intellectuals were for concrete evidence of innate racial differences. Although Odum's dissertation research ultimately contributed little to the discipline of psychology, his work was groundbreaking in the area of folk-music studies because he established new criteria for studying African American folk songs by dividing the songs into two categories, religious and secular. In the first part of the dissertation he discusses religious songs; the second part of his paper deals with the secular songs of blacks. Odum explains that it is his intention to conduct the careful analysis of black folk music that had been neglected in previous studies. Therefore, his dissertation is not merely a catalog of songs but a discussion of common themes, with representative songs as examples. In all, he discusses more than 150 religious songs and fragments and 115 secular songs in the three published articles based on his dissertation.

Odum's interest in the secular songs of Southern blacks was an innovative departure from the work of many previous collectors. He recognizes this neglect and writes that "emphasis has been placed heretofore upon the religious songs, although the secular songs appear to be equally as interesting and valuable" ("Folk-Song and Folk-Poetry" 255). Odum includes a "Brief Bibliography of Negro Folk-Songs" in this published excerpt of his dissertation, which lists twenty-six books and articles dealing mainly with black religious songs. The exceptions are Fenner and Rathbun's *Cabin and Plantation Songs* (1891) and several of Joel Chandler Harris's Uncle Remus collections: these works contain secular songs. Odum was apparently unaware of a number of nineteenth-century articles dealing with secular songs, particularly work songs. At least three articles in Bruce Jackson's collection *The Negro and His Folklore in Nineteenth-Century Periodicals* (1967) describe work songs, including an article entitled "A Georgia Corn-Shucking" by David C. Barrow Jr., Odum's colleague at the University of Georgia (originally published in *Century Magazine* 24 [1882], 873–78).

However, Odum's basic premise is correct: his dissertation is the first collection of American folk song to deal systematically and sympathetically with black secular music. Perhaps Odum found the secular songs more interesting than had previous collectors because he approached the music from a sociological stance instead of a religious one. Rather than seeing the songs as "the vocal expression of the simplicity of their faith and the sublimity of their long resignation" ("Religious Folk-Songs" 7), a view held by many but one that ignored blues and work songs entirely, Odum viewed the songs as a cultural expression, akin to the literature of less oral cultures. "The emotions, the religion, social aspirations and ideals—in fine, the character of a people is accustomed to be expressed in their literature," he writes. "The negro has no literature save that of his folk-song and story" (5). This statement is inaccurate of course, but it is important that Odum saw black folk music as an artistic expression of culture.

Odum devotes the second half of his dissertation, published subsequently in two articles in the *Journal of American Folklore,* to a discussion of secular songs, their singers, language, and themes. He distinguishes between popular "coon-songs" and their adaptations, and songs originating with blacks or "adapted so completely that they have become the common songs of the negroes" ("Folk-Song and Folk-Poetry" 256). He limits his study to the second group, the actual folk songs that have been passed down orally from folk origins, or those popular songs so changed by the singer or singers as to be substantially different from the written or recorded versions. Music scholars always have problems in trying to distinguish between folk and popular music, but Odum at least had an advantage over modern collectors: his informants had only limited access to recorded songs. The songs he collected, therefore, are primarily authentic, orally transmitted folk songs.

Odum divides the singers of secular songs into three types: "songster," or "any negro who regularly sings or makes songs"; "musicianer," or "the individual who claims to be expert with the banjo or fiddle"; and the "music physicianer," or one "who is accustomed to travel from place to place, and who possesses a combination of these qualities." He adds, "Each or all of these terms may be applied loosely to any person who sings or plays an instrument" ("Folk-Song and Folk-Poetry" 259). Odum uses the terms applied to these musicians by blacks themselves rather than using scholarly terminology. This is an important distinction because it brings Odum in line with modern folklorists, who often prefer to use emic or insider terminology rather than etic (external, outsider) terminology in their folklore research. David Evans explains in *Big Road Blues* that Odum used the term "songster" correctly (108). In her book *African Banjo Echoes in Appalachia* (1995), Cecelia Conway finds that the terms "songster" and "musicianer" are still current among black singers (23).

Odum also lists various qualities of African American secular songs: "There is much repetition in both words and music"; the songs "have arisen from every-day life"; and the language "is neither that of the whites, nor that of the blacks, but a freely mingled and varied usage of dialect and common speech" ("Folk-Song and Folk-Poetry" 260, 262, 269). Again, Odum describes traits of black musical performance that have been verified by the research of modern folklore scholars.

Odum concludes his articles on secular music with a bibliography of the songs he has cited and the locale where each song was collected. He does not list the names of individual informants, as any modern folklorist would, but he does distinguish between songs he gathered from residents of the area and those from "visiting singers." The songs were collected from three main groups: residents of Lafayette County in northern Mississippi; residents of Newton County in north Georgia; and gangs on the Illinois Central Railroad in northern Mississippi. He also lists two songs in the miscellaneous category, one reported from Chapel Hill and one from Biloxi, Mississippi (396).

Odum was anxious to publish the book he planned as the first IRSS project, so Johnson set to work editing and rewriting material from Odum's dissertation and folk-song articles. In fact, Odum and Johnson's first collaborative book repeats many of the same songs found in Odum's dissertation and articles, but the second book is based more completely on the collecting of both Odum and Johnson. It also expands on a subject only touched upon in the earlier publications, the work song.

There are only slight differences between the material contained in Odum's folk-song dissertation, his folk-song articles, and the collection *The Negro and His Songs*. Odum's dissertation contained sections that he had to omit from the articles in the *Journal of American Folklore*. He explains: "In order to bring this paper within the scope and limits" of the journal, "it has been necessary to omit the introductory discussion of the songs, for the most part, and to omit entirely the vocabulary and discussion of the mental imagery, style and habits, of the negro singers"

(255–56). The latter discussion is included in *The Negro and His Songs* in a chapter entitled "Imagery, Style, and Poetic Effort." Some of the songs in the collection have titles that are different from those in the articles, and the authors print five songs in the collection from the work of a colleague, Thomas Talley (*Negro Folk Rhymes* 1922). The primary difference between the articles and the collection can be found in the explanatory material. "I was more or less editing a lot of his stuff," Johnson explained. "His style drove me up the wall; I had a few little set-tos with him because he didn't like me tinkering too much with his prose." Still, "in a few months we had put together what you see in the first book" (interview 1985).

Interestingly, a few songs from the *Journal of American Folklore* articles are omitted from the collection. The final lines from one of these songs read: "Then white folks looks like monkeys, / When dey gits old an' gray," and Odum adds the comment that "it must be admitted to be a good rejoinder" and a "powerful comment on the negro's growing sense of race feeling" (266–67). Another omitted song begins, "Don't hit that woman, I tell you why: / Well, she got heart-trouble an' I scared she die" and concludes, "Now, if you hit that woman, I tell you fine, / She will give you trouble all the time" (286). These omissions further support Johnson's assertion that Odum wanted to avoid controversy in this first joint publication, so he removed songs that might disgust white readers.

Unfortunately, the Odum papers in the University of North Carolina Southern Historical Collection do not contain Odum's field notes, so it is impossible to discover whether he was at all selective in his publication of the songs. The collection contains only a few handwritten songs and a few typed song manuscripts with notations in Odum's handwriting where he corrects or add words. Since the collection otherwise exhaustively catalogs Odum's academic life, including his voluminous correspondence, it seems likely that he destroyed his handwritten notes once a song was typed. According to Mary Odum Schinhan, Odum's daughter, his field notebooks have been lost (interview 1985).

## The Negro and His Songs

*The Negro and His Songs: A Study of Typical Negro Songs in the South,* Odum and Johnson's first book, was published by the UNC Press in 1925. Odum's preface discloses the plan for this volume and for future research and publication: "This volume is presented simply as a part of the story of the Negro. Other volumes are planned to follow: another collection of songs brought more nearly up to date; a presentation of song and story centered around case studies; a series of efforts to portray objectively the story of race progress in the United States in the last half dozen decades. In each case the material will be presented simply for what it is and not for cosmic generalizations or ethnic interpretation" (v). He goes on to say that the singers in the book are African Americans but not necessarily representative of all blacks (v). The work is divided into nine chapters. Chapter 1 deals with the African American singer; chapters 2, 3, and 4 describe religious songs; chapters 5, 6, and 7 discuss social songs; chapter 8 describes work songs; and the final chapter focuses on "Imagery, Style and Poetic Effort."

Chapter 2 opens with the statement, "The religious songs of the Negro have commonly been accepted as characteristic music of the race" (14). This chapter repeats much of the information in Odum's dissertation, including a reference to the origin of black folk music: "And while their first songs were undoubtedly founded upon the African songs as a basis, both in form and meaning, little trace of them can be found in the present song: Negro folk produce spontaneous song" (30). This is the authors' only comment concerning the debate on the origin of the African American spiritual. During the late nineteenth and early twentieth centuries, music scholars debated the origins of African American songs, particularly the spiritual. While most scholars recognized both European and African influences on spirituals, as well as the importance of nineteenth-century revival-camp meetings in disseminating the music, the issue of origin is still not completely resolved. Clearly, Odum and Johnson did not want to focus their work on the debate of origin, although Johnson does deal with the topic at length in his later study *Folk Culture on St. Helena Island* (1930).

In some ways Odum's comment that "Negro folk produce spontaneous song" reflects the stereotypical view that black culture is "spontaneous." However, Odum's use of the term clearly indicates he was aware of the improvisational characteristics of black folk song. The terms "natural" and "primitive" seem racist to modern readers, but Odum's understanding of the intuitive nature of African American folk music is an important aesthetic point.

Odum and Johnson also provide one of the earliest descriptions of an African American church service and chanted sermon. Their information is based on a number of black church services that Odum attended when he was collecting songs in 1905 and later in Mississippi and Georgia. Odum recalls a service where "a visiting minister once shouted out . . . 'Oh, the hearse-wheel a-rollin' an' the graveyard opening—ha, ha,' but got no further, for his refrain was taken up by the chorus, and the next day was a new version of the well-known song" (32). Here, Odum accurately describes the typical chanted sermon, including the ejaculatory "Ha, ha" as well as giving readers insights into the composition of variants of folk songs. The authors' discussion of the origins of marching services in the African American church shows their understanding of the importance of rhythm to African American music. They explain that blacks are "passionately fond of dancing" but are forbidden to dance in church, so "marching services were often instituted" as a "substitute for rhythm and excitement of the dance that would satisfy and still be 'in the Lord' " (34).

Chapter 3 lists common themes in black spirituals and three topics related to the theme of sin: victory over sin, the sinner being consumed by sin, and warnings given to the sinner (60). Odum and Johnson do not speculate on reasons for the prevalence of these themes; they merely provide a list and appropriate examples. The three chapters on religious songs (chapters 2, 3, and 4) conclude with a discussion of the largely unsuccessful move by the younger generation to substitute new songs–"standard church hymns"–for the old spirituals in church services (145).

The next section of *The Negro and His Songs* focuses on what Odum and Johnson term "social songs." They speculate on the increasing popularity of blues; perhaps the black folk singer "has finally outgrown that former disposition to sing himself *away from* a world of sorrow and trouble and is coming more and more to sing himself and his troubles *through* that world" (148). Their emphasis here is on the psychological and emotional function of song in black culture.

The authors believe that black secular songs are largely based on personal experience; they recognize both the rich culture and the singers' creativity as sources for the songs. However, their analysis of social songs also reveals their moral bias. They describe songs that "tell of every phase of immorality and vice and filth," in which "the prevailing theme is that of sexual relations"; they conclude that "in comparison with the indecency that has come to light in the vulgar songs of other peoples, those of the Negro stand out undoubtedly in a class of their own" (166). Odum and Johnson remain true to their agenda of social reform even while morally condemning the art of another culture, however, for they attribute the vulgarity not to race but to lower socioeconomic status. The authors claim that these songs give an authentic picture of the lives of Southern blacks, Odum's purpose for collecting in the first place, because "they portray the relation of the singer to his environment; . . . they reflect much of home life and morals, social habits and ideals; . . . and they are themselves testimonial of the creative ability and esthetic sense of the Negro" (159). But, Odum and Johnson warn, "Lest the absence of the higher ideals of home and womanhood, of love and virtue, of industry and thrift, give rise to a pessimistic attitude, it must be constantly borne in mind that this collection of songs is representative only of what may be called the Negro lower class" (159).

In chapter 8 Odum and Johnson enthusiastically describe the work song. They find these songs especially interesting because they combine work with art. The songs are directly related to the work they accompany and the manner of singing is based on a complex leader-and-worker relationship in which "the more efficient the song leader is, the better work will the company do; hence the singer is valued as a good workman" (246–47). The analysis of work songs in this book and their subsequent collection is one of Odum and Johnson's most important contributions to folk-song scholarship. They were among the first scholars to recognize the important cultural information inherent in studying this type of song and especially this performance style, where songs are sung to accompany work. Odum and Johnson include the singers' groaning work sounds in their texts, for example, "Well, she ask me–whuk–in de parlor–whuk, / An' she cooled me–whuk–wid her fan–whuk" (258). In another song, they cite the more common syllable "huh" that accompanies hard physical labor: "The day I lef'–huh–my mother's hous'–huh / Was the day I lef'–huh–my home–huh" (260). Although they were not able to visit Africa and see the origins of the work song, they give accurate and unique descriptions of work-song performance style from early-twentieth-century America.

In the final chapter of *The Negro and His Songs,* Odum and Johnson examine "Imagery, Style, and Poetic Effort." The title of this last chapter is an example of the racism in the book; it implies that black musicians are capable of only poetic effort, not poetic success, but, in fact, the authors find a great deal of poetry in African American folk song. They describe the folk singer's "unusual power to project dramatic scenes into his story," his "concreteness" of detail, the "vividness of his imagination" (269). The essential point in this chapter is that African American folk music is art worthy of detailed analysis and discussion. The songs are an example of the mental imagery of black musicians, their expertise as artists, and the rich cultural background that forms a basis for their talent. This discussion of the artistic quality of African American music and musicians, although somewhat limited in scope, contrasts markedly with the work of many of Odum and Johnson's contemporaries in the field who equated the term "folk" with the appellation "primitive" or "unselfconscious."

## Negro Workaday Songs

Odum and Johnson's second folk-song collection was published in 1926 as the third volume in the UNC Press's Social Study Series, which aimed "to present scientific, descriptive, and objective studies in as interesting and readable form as possible" (ix). Again, the authors express their interest in the songs as social artifacts, "although this indicates no lack of appreciation of the inherent literary and artistic values of the specimens presented" (ix).

The authors clarify their definition of "folk song" in this volume and apologize to students of folk music because in this book they have "frankly taken the position that these semi-folk songs, crude and fragmentary, and often having only local or individual significance, afford even more accurate pictures of Negro workaday life and art than the conventional folk songs" (xi). Of course, contemporary folk-song scholars are grateful that Odum and Johnson accepted such a broad definition of folk songs, because their collections are the only written early source for many songs and fragments. We also understand now that many of these songs are not necessarily fragments but had clear meaning for their intended audience, and that the stanza, not the song, is often the unit of poetry in black folk music. Also, because they approached the songs as sociology, they included many variants and fragments; thus, Odum and Johnson's collections are more "modern" than the collections of their contemporaries that included only "finished" songs. This dichotomy between textual/poetic approaches to folk song and Odum and Johnson's sociological approach is one issue in the debate between literary and anthropological folklorists early in the twentieth century. Contemporary ethnomusicologists appreciate the fact that Odum and Johnson ignored the debate and defined "folk song" in the broadest possible way.

The authors see blues as an important aspect of African American "self-portraiture" because "no amount of ordinary study into race backgrounds, or historical annals of African folk, or elaborate anthropological excursions can give so simply and completely the story of this

Negro quest for expression, freedom, and solace as these low-keyed melancholy songs" (1, 6–7). They also believe that blues are "probably the Negro's most distinctive contribution to American art" (17), a view seconded by many current American music scholars. Odum and Johnson credit W. C. Handy with publishing the first blues, "Memphis Blues," in 1910. As some of the songs Odum and Johnson print were collected as early as 1905, their work is an important addition to blues scholarship if for no other reason than for the number of songs they collected during the early years of the twentieth century.

Odum and Johnson briefly discuss the relationship between folk and popular recorded blues. They explain that the first published blues were based directly on folk songs. But though there are still authentic elements in some recordings, there are also many "new versions" of the blues that are not necessarily folk in origin. However, the folk creative process can also operate in reverse; some recorded songs are adapted by the folk singer so that they actually become folk songs again (23–27). The authors' discussion is especially illuminating because it shows their flexibility in recognizing that the "folk origins" of songs have as much to do with the folk creative process as with an inherited tradition. Thus, in many ways, they anticipate the contemporary emphasis on performance theory in folklore studies.

Odum and Johnson comment on the "seemingly inexhaustible supply of songs among the workaday Negroes of the South. We have yet to find a 'bottom' or a limit in the work songs among the crowds of working men in one community" (14), again emphasizing the innovative and improvisational nature of African American song. The authors classify the 237 "workaday" songs in this book into several thematic categories, although they overstate the genre by considering almost all of the songs "blues." There are blues of the "Lonesome Road," of "Man's Song of Woman," and of "Woman's Song of Man." The book also contains chapters on "Bad Man Ballads," "Songs of Construction Camps and Gangs," "Folk Minstrel Types," and "Workaday Religious Songs."

Although the authors do not identify all of their informants in this collection, they do provide some specific information about the sources of their songs. One song came from "a traveling Negro secretary of the Y.W.C.A." (169), another was sung "with remarkable effect at the Dayton, Tennessee, Scopes trial, with hundreds of whites and Negroes standing around the quartette of Negroes who came for the occasion." The song is "Go 'Long Mule" and includes an appropriate line for that setting: "You can change a fool, but a doggone mule / Is a mule until he dies" (176–77). They explain that the song "I Bid You a Long Farewell" is a particular favorite of one informant, "Aunt Georgia Victrum, age eighty-three, of Jasper County, Georgia." This song and several that follow it in the book "awaken thoughts of the old folk saying their goodby's at the last service of a revival meeting or parting after a long-hoped-for family reunion" (196).

In their discussion of the dynamism of folk music, Odum and Johnson describe the songs of a woman in Georgia known as "Sanctified Mary Harris." The authors comment that although "there seems to be an impression abroad to the effect that the making of Negro spirituals stopped long ago," in fact, every community has its composers (188). As examples, they cite the well-known song "Pharaoh's Army Got Drownded" and then three variations by Mary Harris, who composes her songs when she is "under de spirit" (190).

Odum and Johnson are also careful in this book to cite recorded versions of these songs and citations in other collections such as Sharp's *English Folk Songs from the Southern Appalachians*. Creating such annotations was exhausting work that Guy Johnson obviously felt was important, and these citations certainly make *Negro Workaday Songs* both more scholarly and more useful than the first collection.

Two chapters at the end of *Negro Workaday Songs* point to the direction of Odum and Johnson's future research. Chapter 12 describes "The Annals and Blues of Left Wing Gordon," the informant who later became the source of material for Odum's folk trilogy. In *Negro Workaday Songs* the authors explain that Gordon represents "the workaday songster as a sort of cumulative example of the whole story of the volume" (206), because "it must be admitted that Wing's blues were mixed and of wonderful proportions" (211). The chapter on Gordon is the first collection and analysis of the repertoire of a single African American folk-song informant.

Chapter 13, "John Henry: Epic of the Negro Working Man," reflects Johnson's growing interest in this particular ballad because, he explains, it is "a rare creation of considerable originality, dignity, and interest" and also because it provides "an excellent study in diffusion" (221). Johnson continued his research into the origins of this ballad and published *John Henry: Tracking Down a Negro Legend* in 1929.

Reviews

Odum and Johnson's contemporaries tended to see the folk-song collections as valuable additions to the growing body of literature on African American folk life. Folk-song scholars during the last half of the twentieth century have been more critical. D. K. Wilgus faults the books because they contain only a few tunes and only a few names of individual informants. David Evans, in *Big Road Blues,* finds the books useful only because they contain a large number of songs; essential analysis of the material is lacking.

Together, the two folk-song collections contain the texts of 444 songs, an extraordinary feat in itself. The authenticity of the songs collected is also astounding; as Odum and Johnson say themselves in the preface, "Much of their value lies in the exact transcription of natural lines, words, and mixtures" (*NWS* xi).

The originality of Odum and Johnson's approach in their two collections was recognized and praised by contemporary reviewers. In the *South Atlantic Quarterly* (1925), Newman Ivey White notes the emphasis of *The Negro and His Songs* as "only secondarily a collection of folk-songs; primarily it is a sociological study of the negro as revealed in his songs" (443). He goes on to praise the book as "the best collection of negro songs yet printed," which fulfills its purpose because "whether or not the reader is familiar with the background of Negro life, he will understand it more completely in the light of this volume."

The reviewer notes that only one group of African American songs, the obscene songs, are "necessarily" omitted (444).

Nell Battle Lewis, in the *North Carolina Historical Review* (1925), also likes *The Negro and His Songs* but feels "it is one of the misfortunes of the Negro that most of the mining [of folk material] has been done by whites, for however well-disposed and sympathetic the white man's interpretation of Negro art may be, no one can speak for the Negro as well as the Negro himself" (541). However, "the collection of the songs themselves is valuable, and the evident disposition of the Southern editors to treat the subject thoroughly and sympathetically, if somewhat conventionally, is admirable" (543).

Newman Ivey White's *South Atlantic Quarterly* review (1926) of the later *Negro Workaday Songs* is somewhat mixed. Although the authors have failed to discuss the recent change in African American music and have "neglected to emphasize sufficiently the fact (of which their really extensive study of printed and recorded blues must have made them aware) that this change is in the direction of the Blues" (432), still, the book, more clearly than any other, "sets forth the true Negro laborer as revealed by his songs." "The main object of the book, that of picturing the present-day Negro workman from his songs," White contends, "is most capably fulfilled" (433).

Isabel Gordon Carter reviewed *The Negro and His Songs* in the *Journal of American Folklore* (1925). She writes that the authors "are primarily interested in the social significance of the folk-songs of the American negro in the south. . . . The writers have confined themselves to an analysis of the contents of the songs and a discussion of the attitude and emotions of the negro singer" (624).

Zora Neale Hurston, who was collecting African American folklore during the same time-period as Odum and Johnson, published her book *Mules and Men* in 1935. In a letter to her mentor, anthropologist Franz Boas, where she is reporting on her progress in collecting material, she writes "I find Odom [*sic*] and Johnson in error constantly" (Hemenway 124). In another letter to Boas she claims, "I have been following the works of Odum and Johnson closely and find that they could hardly be less exact. They have made six or seven songs out of one song and made one song out of six or seven. . . . Let them but hit upon a well-turned phrase and another volume slops off the press. Some of it would be funny if they were not serious scientists; or are they" (Hemenway 128).

Of course, Hurston's work has aroused some of the same criticisms as Odum and Johnson's collections because she also conflates material and fails to identify individual informants. Hurston and Boas both assumed that she would obtain more accurate material because she was an African American collecting in her hometown; one of the obvious shortcomings of Odum and Johnson's work is that they were outsiders to the community from which they were collecting. But this problem, on its own, would necessarily negate folklore and anthropology work by anyone other than members of the native group, an issue frequently raised about fieldwork ethics and the subject of a number of recent discussions in the fields of folklore and anthropology.

In addition, Hurston was collecting from all-black communities such as her hometown of Eatonville, Florida, where there was no need for performers to sing in code, and where the songs reflected a more nurturing tradition than that of the itinerant working men who were Odum and Johnson's chief informants. Still, although Hurston had the advantage of an insider's position as a collector of African American folklore, from the viewpoint of a modern folklorist, both Hurston's and Odum and Johnson's work lacks specificity.

Another complaint of present-day folklorists is that Odum and Johnson fail to comment in any depth on an important aspect of African American musical performance: complex rhythms. Although they include a chapter on tunes in *Negro Workaday Songs,* Johnson notes the "utter futility of trying to describe accurately the singing of a group of Negroes when they are at their best" (241), an important acknowledgment of his limitations and the limitations of white musicology at the time. "Any one who has tried to record the music of Negro songs," he adds, "knows that it is very difficult to do more than approximate the tunes as they are actually sung" because of the "slurs and minute gradations in pitch," the variations in subsequent renditions of the same tune, and the "rare harmonies" (242).[1]

However, Odum and Johnson discuss many of the qualities of African American music that present-day scholars have examined in detail. They describe the textual repetition in the songs, the frequency of one-phrase melodies, the function of music as an everyday phenomenon in the culture, and the call-and-response pattern most commonly found in the work songs.

But the main reason Odum and Johnson omit any detailed analysis of the tunes or rhythm of black folk songs is that they were primarily interested in data about the lives of Southern blacks that they believed could be found through analyzing texts of songs. Thus, their work is thematic in focus.

Odum and Johnson's folk-song collections are also problematic as sociology, however. Much of the introductory material and analysis in *The Negro and His Songs* merely serves to perpetuate early-twentieth-century stereotypes of African Americans as lazy and immoral but always musical. As this discussion emphasizes, however, the tendency to generalize about blacks as a group is much less of a problem in the second collection, primarily due to Johnson's greater influence on the content of *Negro Workaday Songs*.

## Contributions to African American Folk-Song Scholarship

The folk-song studies of Odum and Johnson were pioneering scholarship for several reasons. The two were the first academics to pay attention to black secular song, and Odum was one of the earliest collectors of blues. *Negro Workaday Songs* was revolutionary in exploring the work-song repertory. D. K. Wilgus, in *Anglo-American Folksong Scholarship Since 1898* (1959), writes that their analysis of style in African American song was more thorough than that of earlier writers and that they were the first to study the "function" of black songs. They were also the first collectors of black folk song to deal extensively with secular songs. Odum and Johnson's studies of black folk song, in fact, broke fresh ground in British and American folk-song studies by going beyond literary-historical anthologies to a discussion of songs as social and artistic expressions of the life of a people.

In both folk-song collections, Odum and Johnson were primarily interested in the songs they believed provided information about the lives of Southern blacks. Their contribution to folk-song scholarship emerges in the context of the social and psychological functions of the songs. In the second volume, the analysis of folk songs goes beyond their importance as mere curiosities and begins to consider their aesthetic, practical, psychological, and contextual significance.

Both Odum and Johnson recognize the extraordinary artistry of some of the songs they collected. Although the writers still use "the Negro" as a collective term in *Negro Workaday Songs,* their assessment of the singers' artistry shows high praise: "The Negro wastes no time in roundabout or stilted modes of speech. His tale is brief, his metaphor striking, his imagery perfect, his humor plaintive" (22). For example, one song with vivid imagery reads:

> The coon he run so bloomin' fas'
> Till fire come from his heels,
> He scorched the cotton an' burnt the corn.
> An' cut a road through farmer's fiel's. (13)

The authors comment that "there are those who do not feel that the Negro's workaday songs are characterized by the qualities of poetry; yet do they not arouse the feelings and imagination in vivid and colorful language?" (12). They do not comment on the possible use of the word "coon" as code for "black man," but possibly that would have been an obvious point to readers of their day.

A description of a black work song emphasizes both the artistry of the singer and the function of the song. The note to "Bear Cat Down in Georgia" reads, "For sheer artistry, however, one would have to search a long time to find a superior to the following verses, sung by a young Negro workingman, on platform and swing, washing the brick walls of a newly constructed university building" (121). In the song the singer intones: "Lord, I been fallin', . . . . From my place" (122).

The authors recognize that work songs, in particular, serve a practical function, and they explain that "the kind of song is often determined by the nature of the work and the number of workmen" (*NS* 247). Odum and Johnson recall a question they asked a worker once just to see what he would say: "Doesn't this singing hinder you in your work?" The man replied: "Cap'n dat's whut makes us work so much better, an' it nuthin' else but" (*NWS* 52–53).

Odum and Johnson describe the emotional and psychological functions of black folk songs: to express the emotions, dreams, and desires of both the individual singer and the culture as a whole. They provide numerous examples of songs that portray the range of emotional expression in black folk music. They describe the "resourcefulness, humor, defense mechanism, imagination . . . found in the spectacle of a group of Negroes singing over and over again on a hot July day the refreshing lines, 'Oh, next winter gonna be so cold' " (3). Odum and Johnson also write about the "evidences of simple everyday experience, wishful thought, childlike faith, workaday stolidity, physical satisfaction, and subtle humor" in the song "Rainbow Round My Shoulder," which Odum used as the title of his first novel:

I got rainbow
Tied 'round my shoulder,
Ain't gonna rain,
Lawd, ain't gonna rain. (2)

Other emotions are expressed in the songs of the "Bad Man" who "sings sorrowfully of his mother's admonitions and his own mistakes," but "glories also" in the violence of the refrain:

In come nigger named Billy Go-helf,
Coon wus so mean wus skeered uf hisself;
Loaded wid razors an' guns, so they say,
'Cause he killed a coon most every day. (9)

The authors refer to this song in the chapter on "Bad Man Ballads" and explain that the bad man is "no less an artist than the wanderer" (48). They even cite a comment from a preacher who identified Christ "as a man who would 'stand no foolin' wid' " (47). The emotion of these songs includes both humor and pride for a type who is "inexorably drawn into the maelstrom of his day and turned into an inevitable product" (48), Odum and Johnson's remarkably sympathetic view of the African American criminal.

Another emotion the authors describe is the note of "self-pity" that is common in many black folk songs and is nowhere "better expressed than in the forlorn Negro's vision of himself, the last actor in the wanderer drama, folks mourning his death, hacks in line, funeral well provided for" (36, 37). One such song reads,

> Look down po' lonesome road,
> Hacks all dead in line;
> Some give nickel, some give a dime,
> To bury dis po' body o' mine. (37)

The authors seem to have some sympathy for the black singer's "self-pity," especially in the songs of wanderers who are homesick. Not surprisingly, perhaps, many of the songs in this collection come from itinerant construction workers.

Odum and Johnson note the interesting circumstances under which the songs were collected. *The Negro and His Songs* was based on songs collected by Odum in Mississippi and Georgia in the first decade of the twentieth century, but the songs in *Negro Workaday Songs* were collected in the mid-1920s by both Odum and Johnson, many of them in Chapel Hill, North Carolina. Fortunately, new construction work at the university commenced just as they were beginning the second book. The construction projects attracted workers from Georgia, South Carolina, and Tennessee. There were so many workers that the university built barracks, conveniently near Odum's home, to house them. In an interview years later Johnson explained, "Most any day you could go out there on the campus . . . and just hear these gangs singing away while they were digging and shoveling. . . . They had these work songs that were made for digging . . . they'd get into a rhythm passing these things along . . . quite a variety of work songs . . . you'd just sit there by the hour and pick these things up and put them in your notebook." Johnson and Odum could sit on Odum's porch in the evening "and hear singing just across the road really, over in these barracks" (interview 1985). The proximity of this excellent source of musical material led directly to Odum meeting the second person who influenced his work and thoughts on race, John Wesley "Left Wing" Gordon. Also, because Johnson was on the spot collecting both words and tunes from these singers, the second folk-song collection is much more valuable to modern folk-song scholars.

## Johnson's Influence on Odum

Since most of the material in *The Negro and His Songs* was collected by Odum in Mississippi and Georgia before 1910, Odum and Johnson's second folk-song volume, *Negro Workaday Songs,* reflects a combination of more recent songs, more input from Johnson, and a clear change in Odum's attitude toward both the songs and the informants. Several specific, contrasting examples from the two collections illustrate changes in tone and focus between the two volumes, changes that came about as a result of Johnson's influence on Odum's sociology methods and racial views.

In contrast to Odum's survey of African American crime in *Social and Mental Traits of the Negro,* chapter 5 on "Songs of Jail, Chain Gang, and Policemen" in *Negro Workaday Songs* begins with the less judgmental statement: "Not all Negro 'bad men' achieve an abiding place in jail or chain gang. Not all Negroes in jail or chain gang are 'bad men'–not by long odds" (71).

There is also a marked difference between *The Negro and His Songs* and *Negro Workaday Songs* in the treatment of the cultural background material. In the first book, the authors' attempts to explain context often lead to stereotyping. A censorious tone dominates much of the first volume as well. For instance, Odum and Johnson cite some verses of the popular song "Honey, Take a One on Me" in *The Negro and His Songs*. The first verse reads,

> Comin' down State Street, comin' down Main,
> Lookin' for de woman dat use cocain.
> Honey, take a one on me! (193)

The authors then compare "Honey, Take a One on Me" with another song, "I Love That Man, O God, I Do," which also couples love and drugs: "If I thought that he didn't love me, / I'd eat morphine and die" (193–94). The authors claim that, although most of these songs are not suitable for publication, the second song is "more serious and of much better sentiment" than the first, seemingly because drugs are seen as entertainment in the first song but the means of a lover's suicide in the second (193). Odum and Johnson fail to take into account a cultural context for the songs where drugs are prevalent and seen as useful metaphors in songs. But instances of this type of cultural judgment are very few in the second collection, *Negro Workaday Songs*.

Other examples of biased statements in *The Negro and His Songs* include a comment on religious belief: "The Holy Ghost is too vague for the Negro to fathom and is not tangible enough for his imagination" (53), and a reflection on love songs: "There is almost a total lack of any suggestion of higher conceptions of love, married life, and the relations of the sexes" (160). In contrast, the authors open the second book with the important statement that "all examples of folk expression in this volume are left to tell their own story" (ix), with very little sociological explanatory material.

One of the best examples of the change in attitude between the two folk-song volumes is found in an explanatory note in *Negro Workaday Songs*. In a chapter called "The Blues: Workaday Sorrow Songs," the authors add a footnote to comment on the suggestive nature of some blues titles, but in this case they group both whites and blacks together:

> Any one who is acquainted with the slang and vulgarity of the lower
> class Negro will suspect immediately that there are often double mean-

ings in titles like those listed here. Such is the case. Negro song writers and phonograph artists usually have had intimate acquaintance with Negro life in all its forms, and they have doubtless come across many a song which was too vulgar to be put into print, but which had certain appealing qualities. Often a melody was too striking to be allowed to escape, so the writer fitted legitimate verses to it and, if it was at all possible, preserved the original title. Thus it comes about that many of the popular Negro songs of today—and white songs, too, as for that—have titles that are extremely suggestive, and are saved only by their perfectly innocuous verses. The suggestiveness of the titles may also be one explanation of why these songs have such a tremendous appeal for the common folk, black and white. It may be that in these songs, whitewashed and masked though they be, they recognize old friends. (31 n. 1)

Although modern readers might find this comment classist, it is clearly less racist than many of the explanatory notes in *The Negro and His Songs*.

Finally, Odum and Johnson do not comment on specific informants or their fieldwork approach in *The Negro and His Songs*. They clarify their scientific method, however, in *Negro Workaday Songs:* "It is also important to note that in this volume, as in the previous one, all speciments [*sic*] listed, except lines or references otherwise designated, *were taken directly from Negro singers* and do not represent reports from memory of white individuals." They also explain that the book "represents the group of songs *current in certain areas in North Carolina, South Carolina, Tennessee and Georgia,* during the years 1924–25" (x).

Because of these marked differences in the two texts, especially the latter's more careful scientific approach to the material, it seems clear that Guy Johnson's increased editorial influence was instrumental in liberalizing the tone and content of the second volume. In addition, as a passionate musician, he was able to persuade Odum to include some tunes in *Negro Workaday Songs*. As he explained in an interview, "Odum knew no music and had no use for music," an ironic position for a folk-music collector! Thus, although Odum was a pioneer collector of African American folk music, his contributions to the field of ethnomusicology were greatly enhanced by his collaboration with Guy Johnson.

In one of our 1985 interviews, Johnson agreed with critics that his and Odum's research was pioneer work in the field of folklore and that their sociological background influenced the nature of their folklore research. He also claimed that black artists of the Harlem Renaissance benefited from their work. Johnson believed there was a "tendency overall among the blacks to denigrate their own heritage" because of the association of spirituals with slavery, and his and Odum's work "helped recover some of this [heritage] and make it respectable." The development of the Harlem Renaissance at the same time "fitted all right in together with that [their research] and maybe here and there had something to do with stimulating some of these black scholars," for example, James Weldon Johnson and his brother J. Rosamond Johnson. Guy Johnson says "they were very much taken with what we were trying to do and encouraged us."

Some scholars might find Johnson's claims of influence exaggerated, particularly since James Weldon Johnson published *The Book of American Negro Spirituals* in 1925. However, the two Johnsons were friends and Guy Johnson visited James Weldon Johnson in New York. When James Weldon Johnson came to speak at the University of North Carolina in 1927, Odum introduced him to the audience (Johnson, *Research* 36). Also, James Weldon Johnson served as a member of the board of directors of the *Encyclopedia of the Negro;* its "Preparatory Volume" was written by W. E. B. Du Bois and Guy Johnson (1945). While it seems natural for the two Johnsons to be interested in the other's work, certainly James Weldon Johnson did not need help from Howard Odum and Guy Johnson in recognizing the artistry and value of African American folk song. However, Guy Johnson's remark seems to point to the significance of his and Odum's work with *secular* black folk music and the importance to black scholars of focusing on other areas of African American art than just the spiritual.

Clearly, Johnson changed the focus of the important work that he and Odum were doing. Odum's interest in black folk song as a source for understanding culture provided much of the original raw material for the two folk-song collections, but Johnson shaped the material into something very different from Odum's dissertation. In part, Johnson's influence was musical; it seems unbelievable today that Odum collected song texts without collecting tunes, but his practice was not at all uncommon among literary folklorists. Johnson's musical avocation was a great boon to Odum's work, and it certainly makes the second collection more valuable to contemporary folklorists than the first.

The contrast between the writing in the two volumes is also evidence of Johnson's tight editing style. Odum's long, meandering sentences are almost entirely absent from the second volume, and most of the explanatory text focuses on sources for songs and direct literary analysis of the text rather than the sociological generalizations found in Odum's earlier publications on folk song.

However, Johnson's most important contribution to Odum's oeuvre is difficult to document but quite obvious when comparing the two folk-song collections. The material in *Negro Workaday Songs* is presented in a much less racially biased way than the songs in the first collection. Johnson's youth, his more recent sociology/anthropology training at the University of Chicago, and his appreciation of African American singers' musical gifts are all apparent in the second collection. His influence on his mentor is obvious in almost every explanatory sentence in *Negro Workaday Songs*.

Historically, then, Odum and Johnson were pioneers in the study of black folk song, both because of the types of songs they collected and because of their method of treatment. As sociologists who were interested in the style, function, and context of songs rather than their origins or religious or historical value, Odum and Johnson brought a new critical approach to the study of black folk song.

Odum and Johnson succeeded admirably in broadening the study of folk song to include areas previously neglected by literary historians. However, because of their failure to analyze the culture itself, the two collaborative volumes remain most valuable to readers as a collection of a large number of African American folk songs from the early twentieth century. Guy Johnson's subsequent research interests were clearly influenced by his folk-song work with Odum; he would later complete a thorough analysis of a single folk song and its cultural context in his important study *John Henry: Tracking Down a Negro Legend* (discussed in more detail in chapter 5). In addition, in his next folklore project, the Black Ulysses novels, Odum proved that he had learned a great deal about folklore from his younger colleague Guy Johnson.

Odum the collector, in trademark straw hat, in front
of a reconstructed cabin on his farm, ca. late 1920s or
early 1930s. Howard W. Odum Papers, Southern Historical
Collection, Wilson Library, University of North Carolina at
Chapel Hill

Odum, in an Atlanta Bookstore, promoting *Rainbow Round My Shoulder* (published in 1928). Howard W. Odum Papers

Odum and his student and colleague, Guy Benton Johnson, working together in Odum's office at the Institute for Research in Social Science at the University of North Carolina at Chapel Hill, ca. 1930s(?). Howard W. Odum Papers

Original illustrations for Odum's first Black Ulysses folk novel,
*Rainbow Round My Shoulder* (1928). North Carolina Collection,
University of North Carolina at Chapel Hill

Unidentified African American singer from
Odum's files, very possibly John Wesley
"Left Wing" Gordon. Howard W. Odum Papers

Dust jacket for *Wings on My Feet,* the second novel in Odum's
Black Ulysses trilogy and Gordon's World War I memoir,
published 1929. North Carolina Collection, University of
North Carolina at Chapel Hill

Construction of the Wilson Library at the University of North Carolina at Chapel Hill, April 5, 1928. In an interview Johnson explained "Most any day you could go out there on the campus . . . and just hear these gangs singing away while they were digging and shoveling . . . quite a variety of work songs . . . you'd just sit there by the hour and pick these things up and put them in your notebook." North Carolina Collection, University of North Carolina at Chapel Hill

Howard Washington Odum, 1884–1954.
Howard W. Odum Papers

# CHAPTER THREE

# African American Folklore
# in Odum's Black Ulysses Trilogy

ohn Wesley Gordon, the hero of Howard W. Odum's folk-
loristic trilogy, tells a variant of the folktale "The Wonderful
Hunt":

One day John Henry lef' rock quarry on way to camp an' had to go
through woods an' fiel'. Well, he met big black bear an' didn't do nothin'
but shoot 'im wid his bow an' arrer, an' arrer went clean through bear
an' stuck in big tree on other side. So John Henry pulls arrer out of tree
an' pull so hard he falls back 'gainst 'nother tree which is so full o' flitter-
jacks, an' first tree is full o' honey, an' in pullin' arrer out o' one he
shaken down honey, an' in fallin' 'gainst other he shaken down flitter-
jacks. . . . an' after while when he went to git up to go, button pop off'n
his pants an' kill a rabbit mo' 'n hundred ya'ds on other side o' de tree.
An' so up jumped brown baked pig wid sack o' biscuits on his back, an'
John Henry et him too. (*Negro Workaday Songs* 238)

While collecting material for *Negro Workaday Songs,* Odum met "Left
Wing" Gordon. In an interview Guy Johnson described Gordon as a
"real person." Called Left Wing because he had lost his left arm in a
work-related accident after World War I, Gordon was an African American man whom Odum came to know personally. When Gordon was in
Chapel Hill doing construction work, Odum discovered his seemingly
limitless supply of songs and stories. Odum and Johnson published material collected from Gordon in *Negro Workaday Songs,* and later Johnson
included some of Gordon's material in his book *John Henry.* Gordon
was also the prototype of the character Black Ulysses in Odum's folk-
loristic trilogy of novels: *Rainbow Round My Shoulder* (1928), *Wings on
My Feet* (1929), and *Cold Blue Moon* (1931).

Although Johnson helped develop Odum's folklore theory, John Wesley Gordon brought about the most profound change in Odum's thinking on race. It was Gordon's personal knowledge of African American culture that enabled Odum and Johnson to glean real insights from the songs' cultural contexts, a characteristic that distinguished their work from similar studies of the time. Left Wing is the subject of chapter 12 of *Negro Workaday Songs,* a chapter designed, as Odum phrases it, "to present a picture of the workaday songster as a sort of cumulative example of the whole story of this volume": "Here is a type perhaps more representative of the Negro common man than any other. . . . Here is hardship, but withal adventure, romance, and blind urge for survival" (206–7).

Left Wing Gordon claimed to have traveled through thirty-eight states since he was eleven years old, never staying in one place more than three or four weeks. He boasted of at least one blues song for every state. "It must be admitted that Wing's blues were mixed and of wonderful proportions," Odum commented (*NWS* 211). Odum believes Gordon remembers "everything that he has ever heard" (*NWS* 27), including a favorite song:

> You don't know my mind,
> You don't know my mind;
> When you see my [me?] laughin',
> I'm laughin' to keep from cryin'. (27)

Odum explains that this song, "You Don't Know My Mind Blues," is a popular sheet music and phonograph song, but Gordon sings both published verses and some of his own composition. His mixing of "formal and folk material" is characteristic, one of the reasons Odum chose to model his fictional character, Black Ulysses, on Gordon. Gordon's ability to laugh "to keep from cryin'" about the plight of black Americans is also a trait Odum admired.

There seems little doubt that much of the material attributed to the character Black Ulysses in the trilogy was indeed collected from Gordon. Comparisons of songs and statements from *Negro Workaday*

*Songs* tally closely with the same material in the trilogy. In addition, the tone and voice of Left Wing Gordon are closely allied to that of Black Ulysses, although the biographical data on Gordon's life in *Negro Workaday Songs* does not compare exactly with Black Ulysses' life story in the trilogy. Odum describes the work as a "composite autobiography, with every item in it true to fact, and the greater part actual recorded words of the Negro" in a typed memorandum titled "Suggestions with Reference to Black Ulysses Singing" (Odum Papers). In writing the trilogy, Odum clearly recognized the fact that Gordon's race prevented society in general from validating his experiences as important, and he felt he had a mission to clear up misconceptions about the lives and values of African Americans.

Odum's collecting method with Gordon was not unheard of by other collectors of his day. Johnson says that since there were few tape recorders then, "Odum just sat there with a notebook and kept him plied with food and maybe a little bootleg whiskey," while he took notes on Gordon's repertoire (interview 1985). In *Negro Workaday Songs*, Odum asserts that "Left Wing Gordon was and is a very real person, 'traveling man' de luxe in the flesh and blood" (221). Johnson claimed that he "didn't hear him talk enough to know to what extent Odum improved on him with his own imagination" but that some of the material in *Negro Workaday Songs* came directly from Gordon (interview 1985). Odum's close friend and colleague, Gerald Johnson, wrote a congratulatory letter to Odum about *Rainbow Round My Shoulder* where he names Gordon directly and exclaims, "What sedentary white man can fail to feel a twinge of envy of the magnificent vitality of Left-Wing Gordon? In spite of his sufferings and his wallowings, how the fellow had lived!" (January 9, 1928).

When we compare Odum's trilogy to the chapter on Left Wing Gordon in *Negro Workaday Songs*, a scientific rather than a fictional piece, it is apparent that some of the material in the novels came directly from Gordon. For example, some verses Odum quotes in the novels come from songs he attributes to Gordon in *Negro Workaday Songs*. Two verses in the folksong collection read:

O sweet baby, you don't know my min'.

When you think I'm lovin' you, I'm leavin' you behin'.

.  .  .  .  .  .  .  .  .  .  .  .  .  .  .  .  .  .  .  .

Oh, reason I love my lovin' baby so,

'Cause if she make five dollars

She sho bring her father fo'. (216)

These lines are cited in *Rainbow Round My Shoulder* with only slight variation.

The opening of chapter 10 in *Rainbow Round My Shoulder* is also a direct quote from *Negro Workaday Songs:* "I had some mighty fine women. Fust one was Abbie Jones, 'bout Ioway Street. Nex' was in Missouri, Jennie Baker, Susan Baker's daughter. Nex' one St. Louis, lady called Beulah Cotton" (*RRMS* 140; *NWS* 218). In *Negro Workaday Songs,* Odum quotes Gordon as saying he never stays in one place more than three weeks, "leastwise never mo' 'n fo' " (220); in *Rainbow Round My Shoulder,* Black Ulysses claims, "I never stays in one place mo' 'n four weeks, leastwise never mo' 'n five" (8).

However, the biographical data on Gordon's life does not compare exactly with Black Ulysses' life story in the trilogy. Both of Gordon's parents died when he was young (*NWS* 207), but Black Ulysses' mother is a constant and important figure in his narrative. Gordon tells Odum he began traveling at age eleven and is now thirty (*NWS* 208); Black Ulysses began traveling at age thirteen and will soon be thirty-two (*RRMS* 8), but Gordon and Black Ulysses share the same birthday—August 26 (*NWS* 208; *RRMS* 8). Also, Odum's comment in *Negro Workaday Songs* that Gordon had "such experience and adventure as would make a white man an epic hero" (208) shows that Odum was thinking of Gordon's life story as material for an epic.

Although we can trace some biographical data and several songs in Odum's Black Ulysses trilogy to Gordon, at only one point in the trilogy, in the text of *Cold Blue Moon,* does Odum directly refer to Gordon. In this third novel Odum describes a group of workmen telling tales during a rainstorm and introduces "Black Ulysses, the same old

John Wesley Gordon, nicknamed Left Wing Gordon, self-styled alias of 'Wing,' back again from another Odyssey, back at his old job—greatest water boy and helper in America, maybe in the world" (17). Odum waits until the final novel before crediting Gordon at all, although it seems clear that he has been thinking of Gordon all along and using Gordon's material for the three books. Finally giving credit to his primary informant, Odum manifests his development as a folklorist during the years he was writing the trilogy: in the first book he is careful to maintain the fictional identity of his main character; at the end of the trilogy, he credits Gordon in proper folklorist form.

Since Odum's collecting notebooks have been lost, it is unclear exactly which material in the trilogy came from Gordon and which from Odum's imagination. However, Odum's correct representation of the phonology and lexicon of Black English; the authenticity of the folk material in the books, including songs, tales, and beliefs; and Odum's faithfulness to the performance contexts and imagery of black oral folklore point toward Left Wing Gordon as the primary source for the three books.

As I discuss in chapter 2, Odum became more scientific in his approach to folk material largely because of his association with Guy Johnson. Although Odum was the senior member of their collaborative pair, he benefited as much as Johnson did from their mentoring relationship.

The collaboration with Gordon was quite different from the one with Johnson for a number of reasons. In *Negro Workaday Songs,* Gordon claims to be thirty years old (208). When that book was published, in 1926, Odum was forty-two years old and thus Gordon's elder by twelve years. Odum was a highly educated white man, Gordon an uneducated itinerant black worker. On the other hand, Gordon's life experiences were vast and varied. Odum obviously found Gordon impressive as a human being, and he clearly wanted readers to admire the man as he did.

Although Odum does not pretend that his trilogy is as objective as a folklore collection would be, it is apparent from the care he takes with presenting the material that his folklore skills and theoretical approaches developed during the process of writing the three novels. Odum's folklore trilogy is an excellent source of African American folklore from the early part of the twentieth century as well as an interesting study of Odum's increasing understanding of his role as a folklorist.

## Odum's Literary Theory

In his book *Tell About the South: The Southern Rage to Explain* (1983), Fred Hobson asserts that H. L. Mencken and others "saw the beginning of the Southern *literary* renascence in the arrival of a sociologist, Odum, at Chapel Hill—because, Mencken contended and Donald Davidson reluctantly agreed, the new critical spirit, the sociological impulse, strongly influenced Southern literature of the 1920s" (190).

The "new critical spirit" and the "sociological impulse" on which Odum's research was based were undoubtedly important theoretical influences on the writers of the Southern Renaissance. Odum's sociological and folklore research emphasized objective studies of the Southern way of life that could be used as a basis for improving social and living conditions in the South. The work of Southern writers during the 1920s and 1930s is also characterized by a new willingness to recognize and criticize the failings of the South rather than nostalgically praise its virtues.

Studies of the literary aspects of the Southern Renaissance, however, have generally overlooked Odum's own fiction, probably because his writing is not of the same caliber as that of Faulkner and others. Odum's trilogy of novels is interesting, nonetheless, for the insights it can give into the relationship between Odum's sociological theories, his folklore research, and the literature of the South during a period of great change. Despite Odum's occasional stereotypical portrayals of race, two features of these novels make them worthy of study: Odum's use of an oral source as the basis for fiction, and his use of folk material in literature to emphasize the need for social reform in the South. The three novels also provide a clear and valuable record of Odum's changing views on race and the role of folk studies in changing the views of his contemporaries.

Odum describes his own literary theory in his essay entitled "On Southern Literature and Southern Culture" for the volume *Southern Renascence: The Literature of the Modern South* (1953), edited by Louis D. Rubin Jr. and Robert D. Jacobs. Odum was asked to respond to a question posed by Donald Davidson: Why is a writer of the stature of Faulkner the product of Mississippi and the South, if, as the sociologists claim, the South is the most backward region in the United States? In his answer to the question, Odum relates socioeconomic factors and cultural background to the flourishing of Southern literature during the Renaissance (84). Odum begins answering Davidson's question by defining the role and scope of study of the sociologist, who,

> if he is scientific, like the historian of great literatures and the biographers of great writers must understand and portray the total configuration of culture, with all of its interrelationships and interaction with the heritage and behavior of the individual as well as the interlocking causal factors that have made him what he is. On these assumptions the sociologist would predict a Faulkner from Mississippi rather than look to Massachusetts for some or many expected greats. (87–88)

If sociologists look at this "total configuration of culture" in the South, then they must see that "the way of the South has been and is the way of the folk" (88) and folklore is the basis of great Southern literature. Odum describes folk culture as "closely knit, cohesive, nonorganizational, with behavior primarily spontaneous, personal, traditional, yet strongly integrated through its community of growth and moral order. The folk society is thus essentially in contrast to the state society, the one geared to nature and to ethnic and moral structure and the other to technology and to civil organization and specialized structure" (93).

The folk culture of the South provides a foundation for such writers as Faulkner because of its "fourfold heritage" (89). Southern folk culture is "deeply bottomed in the realities of Nature and the frontier struggle, in the heritage of multiple migrant people, in the rise and fall of the upper-folk aristocracy, and in a later powerful race and regional conflict" (88). This definition helps explain Faulkner's achievement on two counts: "In the first place, he has been contemporaneous with the growth stage of a folk-regional culture. In the second place in identifying him with the folk culture of the South we identify him with struggle and travail, in conflict with race, nation, and powerful tradition, fighting for survival for itself and its people" (94).

Odum finds the environmental influences that affected Faulkner consistent with sociological theory, because the sociologist must assume that "all societies grow up and mature in a continuum from the folk culture to the state civilization" (91). The maturation process involves a conflict between "growth, development, and creativeness" and "maturity, standardization, and decay" (91), and conflict is the key to the production of great literature. Odum quotes Moses Hadas, who says "a native theme central in the shaping of ancient fiction was the desire to defend and perpetuate cultural values which were in danger of being lost" (94–95).

Odum believes cultural conflict and a desire to perpetuate cultural values explain the development of a Faulkner in the South. "One cannot imagine a Massachusetts author with so compelling and frustrating environmental pressure as an upsurging source of power as is reflected in a Faulkner page-after-page long sentence reflecting a powerful sympathy, a bitter satire upon the South and the white man, and an eloquent and logical defense of the Southern doctrine, rationalized for the good of the Negro" (97).

The factors Odum describes as responsible for the flowering of Southern literature and the production of a Faulkner are the same factors that influenced Odum's own writing. He too felt the conflict between the folk-cultural values of his youth and the values of the American state civilization of which the South was quickly becoming a part. Odum also had a desire to "defend and perpetuate cultural values which were in danger of being lost," although as a sociologist he believed in the necessary progression from "folk culture to state civilization." He disagreed with the Agrarians and Donald Davidson concerning the future path of the South's development, but his practical attitude did not keep him from having a natural nostalgia for the South of his youth, as well as a desire to understand as much as he could about the people of that South in order to preserve what was best about their culture.

For this reason, Odum's theory of new regionalism and his role as a literary artist were not antithetical. In fact, he believed literature was one important way of "discovering" America, noting, and perhaps explaining, its cultural differences (*Folk, Region, and Society* 196). Singal, in *The War Within*, believes Odum's purpose in writing was to help readers "penetrate beneath external features to the inner characteristics of the South, fostering sensitivity toward Southern problems and capturing some of the majesty Odum beheld in the region's history" (134).

Thus, Odum found a convenient outlet for his theories and feelings about the South in his folklore novels. He used the songs and stories he learned from Left Wing Gordon and other black informants as the material for his three novels, combining sociological theory and folklore research with literature. The first book in Odum's trilogy, *Rainbow Round My Shoulder* (1928), describes the central character, Black Ulysses, and his early life, his work experiences on road gangs and in construction camps, his relationships with women, and his philosophy of life. *Wings on My Feet* (1929) focuses on Black Ulysses' adventures in World War I, and the final book in the trilogy, *Cold Blue Moon* (1931), is a collection of ghost stories and other tales.

## Authenticity of the Folklore in Odum's Trilogy

Because Odum's folklore trilogy contains an enormous amount of authentic traditional material, the novels can give readers important information about Southern black folklore current during the early part of the twentieth century. Odum's increasing awareness of the function of the folklore within the context of Left Wing Gordon's life also shows an important development in his folklore theory.

Although we cannot assess the exact degree of fidelity between the novels and the material Odum collected from Gordon, we do have Odum's testimony that in a more general sense he was trying to be faithful to black oral performance. He asserts in an unpublished document titled "Black Rainbow, Random Notes on MS for *Wings on My Feet*" that Black Ulysses' story "is not told in dialect at all, in the mechanized and technical sense, but in simple folk language of the Negro common man. The rhythm is in sentence and also in paragraph and episode, and set in folk-song and folk-phrase, 'thought and confluence of instinct and emotion' " (Odum Papers).

One test of Odum's fidelity to his informant is, then, whether his representation of black speech seems more accurate than that of such earlier local-color writers as Joel Chandler Harris. We can surmise that Odum's use of black speech came either from his association with Left Wing Gordon and other African American informants or from his knowledge of local-color dialect writing such as that found in Harris's *Uncle Remus* sketches. Because Odum correctly represents Black English in his trilogy, much of the material must have come directly from black informants rather than Odum's imagination or reading. In addition, Odum's novels seem to represent a transition period in the literary representation of dialect.

### Odum's Use of Dialect in the Trilogy

A comparison of passages from *Rainbow Round My Shoulder* and *Uncle Remus: His Songs and Sayings* (1895) clarifies the differences between Odum's and Harris's literary representations of Black English. In Odum's book, Black Ulysses describes an African American church scene:

> 'Nuther thing we got from livin' with grandparents was learnin' speerchials and singin' religious songs. They knowed mo' songs than mama did. 'Co'se all of us knows heap of 'em yet an' lots o' times when we's

lonesome an' blue an' long way from home we still sings 'em. An' they's good workin' songs, too. I knows 'bout all I ever hear 'em sing in church an' learn some besides.

Mighty pretty sight to see ole gray-headed man an' gran'ma, too, singin' in church. Was three colored churches in neighborhood where we live all on hillside 'cep' one which was down in valley. Late evenin' an' night come, Sunday, folks come strollin' in churches, some late an' come from kitchen, an' on prayer-meetin' nights from fiel' and work. Then some one light up church with ole lamp and straighten out seats which been stirred roun' by worshipers. Then mo' worshipers comin' in, an' eve'ything quiet, an' ole folks seem fergit eve'ything in this worl'. Leader opens up wid song, swayin' his body, closin' his eyes, then swingin' his arms an' pattin' his feet, singin' easy an' sof', then high an' appealin'.
(58–59)

A linguistically comparable passage comes from the most famous of Harris's Uncle Remus tales, the story about the "Tar-Baby." The final paragraphs read:

"Skin me, Brer Fox," sez Brer Rabbit, sezee, "snatch out my eyeballs, t'ar out my years by de roots, en cut off my legs," sezee, "but do please, Brer Fox, don't fling me in dat brier-patch," sezee.

Co'se Brer Fox wanter hurt Brer Rabbit bad ez he kin, so he cotch 'im by de behime legs en slung 'im right in de middle er de brier-patch. Dar wuz a considerbul flutter whar Brer Rabbit struck de bushes, en Brer Fox sorter hang 'roun' fer ter see w'at wuz gwineter happen. Bimeby he hear somebody call 'im, en way up de hill he see Brer Rabbit settin' cross-legged on a chinkapin log koamin' de pitch outen his har wid a chip. Den Brer Fox know dat he bin swop off mighty bad. Brer Rabbit wuz bleedzed fer ter fling back some er his sass, en he holler out:

"Bred en bawn in a brier-patch, Brer Fox—bred en bawn in a brier-patch!" 'en wid dat he skip out des ez lively ez a cricket in de embers.
(18–19)

Historically, dialect phonology is represented in literature by misspelling words. If we compare the passages above, it is obvious that

Harris made much greater use of this technique than Odum. In fact, very few of the words in the "Tar-Baby" tale are spelled correctly in Standard American English. *Ears* becomes *years, born* becomes *bawn,* and *says he* is contracted to *sezee.* On the other hand, Odum misspells only a few words: *forget* is spelled *fergit, old* is written as *ole,* and *spirituals* becomes *speerchials.* Otherwise, Odum's primary deviation from Standard English spelling is the use of apostrophes in place of omitted letters in such words as *mos'* and *talkin'.*

Both Odum's misspellings and Harris's local-color style are fairly accurate representations of the phonology of Black English as described by Elizabeth Close Traugott and Mary Louise Pratt in the standard textbook *Linguistics* (1980). In "Tar-Baby" the omission of postvocalic [r] is found in the words *co'se* and *bawn;* the present participle is spelled *settin';* the lack of [T and eth] is illustrated in the words *dat, de,* and *wid;* the reduction of word-final consonant clusters is seen in *roun'.* However, Harris does not omit the word-final [l] in the spelling of *considerbul.*

In the passage from *Rainbow Round My Shoulder,* Odum omits the postvocalic [r] in *mo'* and consistently omits the final [ŋ] from the present participle–*swingin', pattin'.* He omits [Θ and ð] from the word-final position–*wid*–but not in word-initial position–*then.* Odum certainly knew that Black English speakers often omit initial [Θ and ð] because he occasionally spells *that* as *dat,* but he seems to reserve this spelling for special occasions, such as a saying from Black Ulysses' grandfather: "Dat ain't wuth er chew er terbacker" (*RRMS* 58). Odum also represents the reduction of word-final consonant clusters in the spelling of such words as *worl* and *ole,* but, like Harris, word-final [l] is not omitted in *all.*

Harris is much more apt than Odum to misspell vowel sounds, in such words as *en* (in), *ez* (as), and *wuz* (was). These sounds are not necessarily indicative of Black English Vernacular: they are found generally among speakers of Southern American dialect. Odum generally does not misspell vowel sounds, either because he recognized that the schwa [ə] is a Southern dialect characteristic or because he wanted his work to be more readable than that of the local-color writers.

Traugott and Pratt list several important syntactic features of Black English Vernacular, many of them having to do with a different use of the "to be" verb than in Standard English. Geneva Smitherman accounts for some of these differences in *Talkin and Testifyin: The Language of Black America* (1977), by noting that West African languages allow for the construction of sentences without a form of the verb "to be." For example, in Black English, time distinctions are expressed by auxiliary verbs (Traugott and Pratt 331). "He done gone" means "He has gone recently," whereas "He been gone" means "He has been gone a long time" (332). Smitherman describes the be/nonbe rule, or zero copula: "*Be* is omitted if the condition or event is not one that is repeated or recurring. For example, 'The coffee bees cold' means 'Every day the coffee's cold' which is different from 'The coffee cold' which means 'Today the coffee's cold'" (19). Traugott and Pratt also discuss the use of invariant iterative *be* in Black English in such sentences as "Sometime she be angry" and invariant *be* with the function of expressing intention, as in the sentence "He say he be going," which is "also found extensively in white Southern speech" (332). Traugott, Pratt, and Smitherman agree that the various uses of "to be" are the most significant difference between Black English and Standard American English, but this characteristic of the dialect is not found in either Harris's or Odum's literary representations. Their certain association with speakers of the dialect makes it seem unlikely that Harris and Odum were unfamiliar with this trait of Black English. They may have failed to represent this particular characteristic of Black English in their writing because they felt such a significant variation from Standard American English would make their works difficult for white readers to comprehend.

In the passage about the black church service, Odum does deviate from Standard English grammar in several ways: through subject-verb agreement errors—"we's"; sentence fragments—"mighty pretty sight to see ole gray-headed man an' gran'ma, too, singin' in church"; and omission of articles before nouns—"Leader opens up wid song." All of these variations from Standard English, however, could just as easily represent casual speech or the Southern American dialect. Other important syntactic traits of Black English such as the use of *It's a* instead of *There's a,* multiple negation, and question transformation are not represented in Odum's trilogy (Traugott and Pratt 333–34).

Concerning lexical evidence of Odum's knowledge of Black English, he uses few words in the Black Ulysses trilogy that are distinctive to Black English. However, Black Ulysses' speeches often contain profanity, a characteristic of Black English that Smitherman discusses. She believes the frequent use of profanity by speakers of Black English does not always represent a desire to "cuss somebody out"; the words can be used both negatively and positively or merely as fillers.

One example of Black Ulysses' use of profanity is found in *Rainbow Round My Shoulder* when he describes the conversation of a man and a woman fighting: "Don't you never speak to me no mo', you ole mucker-tucker, 'cause I don't give a goddam about you nohow. You run 'round with every ole nag in town an' then want to raise hell with me" (162). Odum's willingness to use profanity in spite of the possibility of offending readers may show an understanding of its place in the vocabulary of Black English, or this (and other examples of profanity in the books) may be a direct quote from Left Wing Gordon or other informants. "Mucker-tucker" is obviously a substitution for what Smitherman calls "the black lexicon's most famous word" (60), and Odum's use of a variation may show his familiarity with some of the lexicon of the dialect as well as his unwillingness to use the stronger term.

According to Traugott and Pratt, in their discussion "Stereotypic versus Variable Representation of Language Varieties" in literature, the weakest representation of dialect is found in the use of spelling errors in such words as *ennything* or *wimmen*. The use of phonological-morphological markers like *runnin'* or lexical forms like *ain't* is higher on the scale of authentic representations of dialect (339). Odum is probably a transition figure in the area of dialect representation in literature. He uses only a few spelling errors and phonological-morphological markers to represent dialect. Odum accurately represents the phonology of Black English in his trilogy, and there is some evidence that he understood something of the lexicon of the dialect. However, since Odum could have obtained knowledge in these areas from reading local-color writers, and since he does not attempt to represent syntactic features in his books, it is not certain from linguistic evidence alone whether the novels come from direct transcriptions of folklore informants such as Gordon.

A marked difference appears in Odum's general attitude toward Black English in the three books. *Rainbow Round My Shoulder* is based on a number of first-person accounts from Black Ulysses, quite a few songs that he sings, and each chapter contains an opening section that is written in Standard English rather than dialect. These sections are obviously intended to represent the author's thoughts on the material he collected from Gordon, and they may also show an honest attempt on Odum's part to recognize the contributions of his informants by separating his words and theirs. Unfortunately, he does not always manage graceful transitions between Standard English and Black English sections, and at times the chapter openings seem intrusive because they invariably give readers a picture of a white man looking in at black culture. That picture, though sympathetic, is necessarily distant, and not always understanding.

However, in the next novel, *Wings on My Feet,* Odum chooses to omit any Standard English sections; the novel consists entirely of Black Ulysses' first-person account of his adventures in World War I and some song texts. It seems significant that Odum allows his character, and perhaps the real Left Wing Gordon, to speak for himself in this second book. Here, "translating" for the informant seems unnecessary in the face of the power of his story. As a result, this book is much more interesting from both a literary and a folklore point of view.

In the final novel, *Cold Blue Moon,* Odum returns to the format of Standard English openings to each chapter followed by stories in dialect told by Black Ulysses. In chapter 4 I discuss his possible political and commercial reasons for such a change. Still, this third novel contains more authentic folklore—from a number of possible sources—than the other two novels, and as such it represents the pinnacle of Odum's career as a collector and disseminator of folk material.

## Odum's Use of Black Expressive Forms in the Trilogy

Odum's accurate use of Black English Vernacular varies so much in the three novels that perhaps a more accurate means of assessing the authenticity of the materials in Odum's work is to examine the trilogy for traditional black expressive forms. Odum's inclusion of such forms indicates his first-hand familiarity with black oral genres.

Smitherman describes a distinctively black mode of discourse called "signification," which "refers to the verbal art of insult in which a speaker humorously puts down, talks about, needles–that is, signifies on–the listener" (118). She notes that a common subject for an exchange of insults between blacks concerns some of the distinctive physical characteristics of African Americans. One term, "nappy," describes kinky hair. This term once had a derogatory meaning, according to Smitherman, but it is now a neutral term (64). In *Rainbow Round My Shoulder,* Black Ulysses engages in a highly personalized exchange of insults:

> Yo's head's so nappy it stop ever clock from runnin'. Say, ole nigger, if I was to cut off yo' hair an' put it in a bottle, it rattle lak shots.
>
> You needn't be talkin', you ain't got 'nuf hair on yo' head to wad er musket.
>
> Gwa'n, nigger, you ain't got no sense; if I was to ketch hold o' one stran' o' yo' hair an' pull, I'd ravel yo' whole brains out. (31)

Black Ulysses calls this verbal fun "joreein' " (30). In his book *Talking Black,* Roger Abrahams distinguishes between playing the dozens, another mode of black discourse that involves insulting someone's mother, and signifying, or insulting the person directly. It is important to note that Black Ulysses describes the tone of "joreein' " as amiable rather than hostile. He says, "Mos' time we don't mean nothin' joreein'" (30). This fits with the context of signifying, a kind of verbal fun, which, as Smitherman points out, is not meant to be taken seriously (119). According to this definition, Black Ulysses' "joreein'" might be the same as signifying. Smitherman lists a term that is somewhat synonymous with signification: "joanin" (119). Perhaps "joreein'" and "joanin" are variations of the same word. Odum also uses the word "joree" as part of the title of a chapter on tall tales, emphasizing the quality of exaggeration suggested by the term. In any case, Black Ulysses' display of signifying ability in a similar context to that found among modern black speakers provides evidence that Odum was quoting in this case from his black informants.

Smitherman also comments on the use of the word "nigger" by blacks. When used by whites the term is always an insult, but when used by blacks it may be "a term of personal affection" or "a way of expressing disapproval of a person's actions"; it may mean "culturally black" or it "may simply identify black folks," in which case it has a neutral value (62).

Another example of African American oral tradition is the bragging speech. Black Ulysses is quite adept at the genre that Smitherman calls "boastful raps," used for the purpose of verbally "conquering foes and women" (82–83). Smitherman provides an example of the boastful rap from Hubert Rap Brown's autobiography *Die Nigger Die!* (1969):

> Man, you must don't know who I am.
> I'm sweet peeter jeeter the womb beater
> The baby maker the cradle shaker
> The deerslayer the buckbinder the women finder
> Known from the Gold Coast to the rocky shores of Maine
> Rap is my name and love is my game. (82)

Black Ulysses uses a similar tone when he describes the way he feels when he is drunk:

> Well, I'm some red shadow myself when I gits my sheer roastin'-ear milk. Like I said I can sho' step on my box when I'm fohty with de cleaver. . . . When I'm half split 'bout high as Georgia pine, goddam, I

> can peep through muddy water an' see dry land. Jes' let me git alcohol
> behind my eyes, good-God-a-mighty I'm right wid the world, rockin' in
> the slime. (*RRMS* 129)

I could find no exact parallels between Black Ulysses' boastful raps
and those collected by folklorists since Odum, but the similar style indicates that Odum was familiar with the form. He may have chosen to
edit some of the obscenity from Left Wing Gordon's raps, an assertion
supported by an unpublished list from Odum's files, "Suggestions with
Reference to Black Ulysses Singing." In the list of ideas Odum notes
possible problems with the manuscript, including "Dialect, obscene or
objectionable language, objectionable words to Negro, like 'nigger'"
(Odum Papers).

Odum was also familiar with the black "bad man" hero, Stagolee,
a character in a famous "toast," another African American mode of
discourse. A description of Stagolee as having a "tombstone disposition and a graveyard mind" illustrates this type of speech performance.
Odum includes an excerpt from a song about Stagolee in the trilogy,
which Black Ulysses introduces by saying "Stagolee must 'a' been bad
man 'cause he was always out for finish fight an' always got his man
an' lay po' body down" (*RRMS* 190). Then he sings:

> Stagolee was bully man, an' eve'ybody knowed,
> When see Stagolee comin', give Stagolee road,
> Oh, that man, bad man, Stagolee done come. (*RRMS* 191)

The same verse can be found in *The Negro and His Songs* (196–97),
so it is clear that Odum obtained it from a black informant. The song
bears no resemblance to the toast about Stagolee, which has a definite
plot, but the description of his character rings true. The term "bad man"
in Black English has a positive connotation, whereas in Black Ulysses'
introduction of Stagolee as a "bad man," the tone seems condemning.
This passage may be an example of Odum completely misunderstand-
ing the tone of certain aspects of the authentic black folklore he used
in his trilogy.

When we compare Odum's trilogy to folklore collections based on a black informant, it becomes more evident that Odum obtained his material from one or more authentic folk sources. Besides including Black English modes of discourse in his trilogy, Odum also makes use of other black folklore genres.

## Odum's Use of Rhymes, Hoodoo, and Beliefs

Another example of authentic black folklore in Odum's trilogy is found in his use of folk rhymes. Some of the rhymes found in the trilogy are also found in Newbell Niles Puckett's *Folk Beliefs of the Southern Negro* (1926). Puckett attributes a conjure rhyme to Odum's article "Negro Hymns" (*Journal of American Folklore* 26 [1913]). Odum's later version of the rhyme in *Rainbow Round My Shoulder*—"Ole Satan is liar an' conquerer, too, / If you don't min' gwine conjure you" (56)—may contain a misprint because the rhyme he cites in "Negro Hymns" and the one quoted by Puckett reads: "Ole Satan am a liah an' a *conjurer* too: / Ef you don't mind out he'll conjure you" (168). In fact, in a letter to Odum, the well-known African American sociologist Charles Johnson cites the word "conquerer" as an error (January 4, 1928).

Another rhyme from Puckett is also found in *Rainbow Round My Shoulder:*

Her face look lak a coffee-pot
Her nose look lak de spout,
Her mouf' look lak a fiah-place
Wid de ashes taken out. (76)

Puckett attributes this rhyme to Mr. Harland Wallace of Carthage, Mississippi (602). Odum uses a rhyme that is almost identical in *Rainbow Round My Shoulder:* "Yo' face look lak a coffee-pot, yo' mouth look lak the spout, yo' nose look lak the fireplace wid de ashes pokin' out" (31).

Odum's trilogy also contains numerous folk beliefs, particularly in *Cold Blue Moon,* for which he may be indebted to Puckett. For example,

Puckett describes the belief that "if a person dies hard it is a bad sign; he will haunt the survivors" (81). In *Cold Blue Moon,* Black Ulysses comments that Old Mistis "must 'a' died hard on account o' so many ghosts ha'ntin' place where she been" (245). Similarly, Puckett writes that "if a horse neighs twice after midnight when his master is sick the master will die" (476) and that the hooting of an owl is a death omen (482). Black Ulysses says in *Cold Blue Moon* that the morning after "folks kept hearin' screech owls an' heard hoss neigh two times after midnight," Marse James was found dead on his front porch (228). Several beliefs regarding ghosts are also common to both Puckett and Odum. Puckett comments that ghosts often congregate in churches "which is made known by lights in the church" (116); Black Ulysses describes a man who finds a church with "lights all blazin'" and haunted by ghosts (*CBM* 144). Puckett describes "double-sighted" people who can see ghosts (137), and one of Black Ulysses' stories tells of Uncle John's unique ability to see spirits (*CBM* 241–42). A common motif in ghost stories is speaking to the ghost with such phrases as "What in the name of the Lord do you want?" (Puckett 140); Odum uses this motif several times in *Cold Blue Moon* (238–43).

Odum also describes some folk beliefs associated with hoodoo. Zora Neale Hurston, in *Mules and Men: Negro Folktales and Voodoo Practice in the South* (1935), explains the importance of black cat bones in hoodoo and describes a ceremony for selecting the correct bone by boiling the cat and passing the bones through her mouth until one tasted bitter (221). Puckett describes a similar ceremony where the person should pass the bones through the mouth while looking into a mirror. He writes, "When you get to the right bone the mirror will become dark" (257). Puckett also notes that "others say the cat should be cooked in a graveyard and the bones thrown into running water. The one that will go upstream is the proper one" (258).

Black cat bones are also important in Odum's trilogy. As a gambler, Black Ulysses has faith in the lucky combination of black cat bones and dice and believes that the hero of the tale "Blue Jim and Black Buzzard" must have had three black cat bones because he was able to win the most impossible bets (*RRMS* 12, 217). Black Ulysses describes a fairly elaborate ceremony for choosing the correct black cat bone, which not only involves Puckett's ceremony of finding the bone that will swim upstream but also swearing "by all the gods that made you that what is between yo' two hands belong to the devil"; then, "anything you want to do you can do" (*RRMS* 13).

Odum's use of black folk beliefs in the trilogy that have been documented by both Puckett and Hurston points to the authenticity of his folk material; however, Odum does not footnote any sources for these, and since there are no folk beliefs in the trilogy that are exact quotations from Puckett, it may be that each collector received similar information from different informants. Although Odum's indebtedness to black beliefs reported in Puckett's book cannot be proved, several of the story motifs in *Cold Blue Moon* seem likely to have come from Puckett. One story in Puckett tells of a little boy who

> cursed and swore at an old hired lady on the place because she was smoking his father's pipe. Shortly afterwards the old lady died. All went well until about three weeks later when the lad awoke one night shrieking that the old lady was after him. His parents went to the rescue but could see no one, though the sheets, quilts, and window curtains in the room were tearing themselves, a strip at a time, and tying themselves about the boy's neck, arms and legs, almost choking him to death. All they could do was to cut the strips as fast as they were tied until the invisible Something left for the night. (124)

Black Ulysses also tells of a boy who has a frightful experience one night when

> sumpin' else come in dark room, jumped on bed, and so they started fightin' all over room, all round an' round. So finally somehow this little boy gits up on old mantelpiece. So they fit an' fit. Boy could feel cold air an' see figures round an' round, but didn't make no sound. Can't say how long boy hung up on mantel skeered to death, but finally let out turrible yell till white folks come. Thought doors an' winders were wide open, bed wus broke all to pieces, an' wus blood on floor. Said that boy

never did git over skeer. Told me wus room where quality folks been gamblin' an' drinkin' an' some wus killed in fight or sumpin'. (*CBM* 31)

Puckett also paraphrases a story originally found in *Southern Workman* (1894) about a man driving a buggy past a graveyard at night. He sees nothing but knows something is getting into the buggy beside him because

he could hear the springs creak and feel them settle under the weight. The horse moved on very slowly; nothing could persuade him to go faster. The unhappy man tried to sing, but could think of no other song than "Hark from the tomb a doleful sound." His unseen companion mocked him, "Hark! Hark! Hark!" He could feel the mouldy breath of the visitor on his shoulder. When the man and his ghoulish companion neared a store the horse stopped and the unseen visitor left him without a word of thanks. (121–22)

Black Ulysses tells a similar story in *Cold Blue Moon* with the same singing motif. A man is driving a buggy and he

feels one side of buggy saggin' down an' hears screakin' lak somebody sholy getting' in beside him. Can't see nobody, can hear 'em. Sweat pourin' off face. Tried to sing, can't sing; tried to whistle, can't whistle. So then hoss goes on 'cross creek an' up-hill. Thought he could feel cold air an' felt like somebody peerin' round lookin' in his face. Tries to make hoss go faster; can't do it, hoss jes' pokes 'long. So when hoss gits to top of hill, stops suddenly, neither will he go on. 'Bout that time, buggy screaks an' side where ghost been settin' lets up an' hoss goes on. (250–51)

Another of Puckett's tales describes a "slave-owner who used to put a sheet over his head and go out and scare his slaves" (131). The story continues:

This man owned a monkey who was very imitative. One night the monkey watched him put the sheet over his head and slip out to scare people, whereupon the monkey slipped a sheet over his own head, and, unobserved, followed his white master. The man hid behind a tree and when a Negro passed he jumped out to scare him. The Negro ran; then the sheeted monkey jumped out from behind the white man, and the white man ran with the monkey after him, calling, "Run big Jim; little Jim ketch you!" (131)

Black Ulysses attributes similar antics to Marse James in *Cold Blue Moon.* James also owns a monkey and he

tells one of old slaves to go down to field near graveyard an' git him some weeds, says he wants to give medicine to monkey. So he puts on white sheet an' slips round by graveyard, gonna skeer old man. How- somever, monkey been trained to do like his marster and so he gits lit- tle sheet an' slips 'long behin' Marse James an' sets down where can't be seen. So when old slave comes, Marse James starts runnin' after him an' monkey starts runnin' after Marse James. So he looks round an' sees lit- tle white ghost comin' out of graveyard, an' bein' 'bout high as Georgia pine, he don't know whut to make about it. So they both keep runnin' and slaves hollerin' "Run, big Fred, little Fred ketch you; run, big Fred, little Fred ketch you." (64–65)

Odum's trilogy is rich in African American rhymes and beliefs that he may have obtained in part from Puckett and in part from his own informants, including Left Wing Gordon. Although he apparently saw no need to document sources in a fictional work, the three novels are still valuable resources for material current among African Americans in the first third of the twentieth century.

## *Folktale Genres Found in the Trilogy*

Odum's in-depth knowledge of a number of important African Amer- ican folktale genres, including tall tales, ghost tales, trickster tales, and Marster and John tales, also points to the authenticity of the folk ma- terial in the trilogy. Again, parallel versions of many of these stories can be found in documented collections of African American folklore. The versions from Odum cited below are some of the earliest collected examples of many of these tales among African Americans; thus, the trilogy is also an important source of comparison for subsequent collectors. Finally, Odum's extensive use of folktales in the last volume of the trilogy, *Cold Blue Moon,* underscores his increasing maturity as a folklorist. Odum began to see the need for preserving this important material for its artistic value rather than merely as a source for understanding the culture of African Americans.

In the trilogy, Black Ulysses tells two tall tales that have parallels in folklore collections from both black and white informants. Chapter 14 of *Rainbow Round My Shoulder* is titled "Tall Tales and Joree Jaw" and includes a succession of lies and tales. One tale reads:

> Well, talkin' 'bout rabbits 'minds me I had a dog once run so fas' run into a tree an' split hisself wide open. I took an' put him back together, but I done went an' put him back wrong–I put two feet up an' two down. But I couldn't change hit. Well that dog run till he got tired on two feet an' then he doan do a thing but turn over an' run on the oder two–sho 'nough. (199)

Leonard Roberts, in his collection of Kentucky mountain folktales entitled *South from Hell-fer-Sartin* (1964) cites a similar version of this tale from a white Appalachian informant.

> One time I figured I wanted to go a-hunting up North. I went up in Alaska. I had the best dog I ever owned in my life. That dog was so fast he would jump a rabbit and have it half dug out before it ever got to the hole. So one day he jumped a red fox. So I figured right there the boy had struck his match. He run into a tree and split hisself wide open. I got to him just as quick as I could. I was in a hurry, you see, and I slapped him together and I got two legs up and two legs down. Well, he would run on two legs a hundred yards and he'd run on the other'ns a hundred yards back. And he froze hisself to death a-running from one of them trees to the other–just a hundred yards between 'em, you see. (145)

In her thesis "Howard Cotton: A Black Teller of Tall Tales" (1981), Joan Fenton notes that another black tale-teller, Willie Brooks, told her a tale about a hunting dog "sawn in two and put back together with two feet up and two down" (49).

Another set of tall tales found in Odum's trilogy includes variants of a tale listed as number 1890, "The Wonderful Hunt" in the Aarne-Thompson index, *The Types of the Folktale* (1928). One tale in *Rainbow Round My Shoulder* reads:

I went out once ahuntin', never had nothin' but a Winchester rifle, six-teen shot. Goin' out to see how much game could I kill with sixteen balls. My dog jumped a deer goin' round a big mountain. Every time he gits over against me I'd make a smack at him comin' round mountain, and when ball hit side o' the mountain he'd be one hundred yards ahead, me shootin' square at his side too. I shot at him fifteen times, but the las' time I shot at him I shot right in behin' him. An' him an' the ball took twenty-five circles round mountain 'fo' ball caught up wid him. He got round 'gainst me an' I seed him tumble. Then I goes up on the river an' found some wild pigeons. I never had but the one ball, but I wanted to kill all the pigeons. I studied and studied how to kill 'em all. So I shot at the limb they's settin' on, an' that split the limb an' caught they feet in it. Then I had to climb the tree to cut limb off. An' in cuttin' it off they fell in river. I caught 'em all but one. An' in swimmin' round in there after that one I caught my bosom full o' fish. So full o' fish it bust button off the top o' my shirt and killed rabbit on bank in brush-pile. Then I throwed rabbit over in broom sage an' killed whole covey partridges roostin' there with heads together. (199–200)

A competing version of the tale by another teller follows; it is based on a hunt with a musket. The speaker kills a turkey and then

the ramrod went 'cross and stuck through a tree an' killed it, half of the barrel went down-river an' killed a drove of geese, the other half went up-river an' killed a drove of ducks. The hammer, hit flew off an' killed a squirrel up in a tree, and the lock it blowed off and killed a lion comin' after me. The gun kicked me back on a rattlesnake an' me stompin' round there, that killed it, kicked my coat off an' smothered a bear to death so I thought I was best marksman in the worl'. Got all that game at one shot. (201)

Roberts cites a variant of this tale told by a white informant, which reads in part:

> I had a rifle-gun, had one round of ammunition. I looked out in front of me and there laid a rattlesnake about twelve feet long. Well, I started to shoot it and about that time I heard a noise down the river. I looked and there was 5,000 wild ducks comin' up the river. Well, I didn't know which to shoot, the ducks or the rattlesnake. About the time I started to shoot the ducks I heard another noise up the river and I looked and there was 5,000 wild geese. Well, I shore didn't know what to do then. I knowed I couldn't kill the geese and the ducks, all, and the snake. So I said to myself, "I'll kill the snake and try to catch a goose as she passes." I pulled the trigger. The barrel busted. Half of it went down the river and killed 5,000 wild ducks. The other half went up the river and killed 4,999 wild geese. . . . Well, I had all them geese and ducks and started across that bridge, and the bridge broke with me. Down I went twenty feet deep in the water. I swimmed, I kicked, and I paddled, and when I finally got to the bank and got out I had 300 pounds of fish in my hip boots. (147)

Richard Dorson, in *Negro Folktales in Michigan* (1956), includes a variant of this tale told by black informant J. D. Suggs:

> Fellow went out hunting. He didn't have but one shell. And he happened to look up, and first thing he seed was ten ducks sitting on one limb. He looked over to one side before he shot, and saw a panter standing there. He looked over on his left–there was a big buck standing there. He looked behind, and there was a covey of partridge right behind him. He didn't know which one to shoot at. He looked straight in front of him and he seed a big bear coming towards him. He knowed he had to shoot the bear, for the bear would kill him–he knowed that. So he cocked both muzzles of a double-barreled muzzle loader, pulled both triggers the same time. The shot killed the bear. The ramrod shot out and hit the limb and caught the ducks' toes before they could fly away. And the hammer on the left, it flew off and killed the deer. The right hammer, it

flew off and killed the panter. He kicked his overcoat off, and smothered the covey of partridges. (177)

Another variant of "The Wonderful Hunt" is printed in Zora Neale Hurston's book *Mules and Men* (1935), not a documented folklore collection but one containing authentic material based on her personal knowledge of black folklore (115).

The best proof of Odum's indebtedness to black oral tradition for his material occurs in *Negro Workaday Songs,* where Odum and Johnson include a tale about John Henry, with the note "This story was recorded at Chapel Hill, N.C., but, as far as we can tell it came originally from Stone Mountain, Ga. It is given as nearly as possible in the words in which it was told" (238 n. 1). The first paragraph of the story is a variant of "The Wonderful Hunt" but with John Henry as the hero rather than the speaker (see chapter opening). Johnson also included the tale in his book about John Henry with the introduction: "The only really bizarre tale I have ever heard about John Henry is one which Professor Howard W. Odum obtained from a construction-camp Negro at Chapel Hill three years ago" (144). It seems clear that Odum obtained at least one authentic version of this tale from a black informant, probably Left Wing Gordon, and he may have adapted the tale himself in *Rainbow Round My Shoulder* or included other variants of the tale that he collected from other informants.

Odum includes another common folktale type in his trilogy, ghost tales. The text of *Cold Blue Moon* is based largely on ghost tales narrated by Black Ulysses; several of these stories are variants of tales collected by other folklorists. One tale reads:

I heard tell 'bout preacher wus offered so much money would he stay in ha'nted house all night. So he goes an' takes Bible an' sets down important like an' opens up Bible an' begins to read. 'Bout that time first ghost comes sneakin' in like hot air or maybe like cold breeze an' wet, look lak man only ain't got no head, 'scusin' if he have head ain't got no body, else if he have body ain't got no arms. So he says to preacher, "Is you gonna stay here till Whalem-Balem comes?"

Ole man so skeered he don't say nothin'. So nex' ghost come in he look lak mule, maybe old gray mule only he ain't got no head neither, 'scusin' if he got long-eared head, ain't got no body. So he says to preacher, "Is you gonna stay here till Whalem-Balem comes?"

Still the old man so skeered he don't know whut to do; thinks maybe he better be goin', neither can he move. So 'bout that time, third ghost comes in, look lak cat, only biggest cat anybody ever seen, got red eyes lak fire and spittin' and mewin' like red-hot stove or sumpin'. So he meows, "Is you gonna stay here till Whalem-Balem comes?"

'Bout that time old preacher ain't got no voice an' feel mighty sick at his stomach and decided maybe he better make him little coffee and fry some meat. So he does. 'Bout time he be ready to drink his hot flambotia strong, fo'th ghost comes in, look lak dog, only got big tushes lak boar. So he reaches down an' et up all meat an' lap up all coffee. He then snaps up at preacher with tushes all showin' an' like impudent snarl, maybe snappin' teeth together like wolf, "Is you gonna stay here till Whalem-Balem comes?"

So old preacher hollers, "Hell, no, I'm done gone." (22–24)

This story is followed by several tales where increasingly bigger and bigger cats scare people out of haunted houses (24–30).

Dorson prints a variant of this tale told by Joe D. Heardley and called "Rufus in the Hanted House." This version describes a man who built a new house but could not get anyone to live in it, until he offered $250 to anyone who would stay there overnight. One man volunteered and was feeling certain of his money, but while he was sitting there

a little cat come through a little hole in the door, walked up to him, walked around, touched him on the leg, and asked him, "Are you going to stay here till Rufus comes?" So he run the little kitten out, pulled his hat back over his eyes. Then a little monkey come in, commenced to playing all around the house, hopped up on his knees, looked in his eyes, and asked him, "Are you going to stay here till Rufus comes?" He took his pistol out, stuck it in the monkey's ears, his nose, his eyes, told him he'd blow his brains out if he didn't get out. Out the monkey went. He pulled his hat back over his eyes.

And a big gorilla walked in, knocked the door down, and touched him on the shoulder. He opened his eyes and the gorilla asked him, "Are you going to stay here till Rufus comes?" So then he moved the gorilla over out of his way, busted the pound heap of lard on the skillet over the log heap of fire, broke the three dozen eggs in the skillet, throwed the slab of sowbelly in the skillet and fried and eat that. Then the gorilla walked up to him, touched him on the shoulder and said, "Say, Buddy, is you going to stay here till Rufus comes?" Then he taken his pistol out and showed it to the gorilla and told him he'd kill him if he didn't get out. So then the gorilla reached in the log heap of fire, pulled out the skillet, and drank all the hot grease. Then he threw the skillet back in the fire. Next he reached over and got one of those red hot charcoals, and commenced to clean his teeth. So then he touched this fellow on the shoulder again and said, "Now, this is the third time I asked you, is you going to stay here till Rufus comes?" He said, "No, Rufus is here now." And he left. (129)

Another ghost tale in *Cold Blue Moon* describes dogs treeing a ghost. The hunters hear a strange sound and decide to cut the tree down. The end of the tale reads, "So when boys wus 'bout half-way through cuttin' tree sumpin' come slidin' down tree so savigorous till dogs begin bristlin' and whinin' an' turn tail an' run like hell, yelpin' an' howlin' " (176).

Fenton summarizes a similar tale told by Howard Cotton:

Every time Howard went to hunt by the graveyard, the dogs would strike. This time they treed at a big oak, but when he shined his light up there, he didn't see anything. But whatever it was, it was making "the queerest fuss," sounding like a baby crying.

Next the dogs treed at a small tree and again he couldn't see anything. Then they treed a third time and when Howard shined his light, he saw eyes looking at him. He shook the tree and it fell, and the dogs jumped on it, but there wasn't anything there. Howard decided it wasn't "nothin' but haints," and went on home. (56)

A common ghost-tale motif is the ghost that reveals the location of buried treasure (E371). This motif is found in a series of tales in *Cold Blue Moon* that Black Ulysses introduces by saying:

Wus 'nother kind o' ghost story folks told a heap of. Like I said, endurin' the war with Yankees southern folks would hide valuables. Faithful old slaves would hide valuables of white folks an' maybe would die befo' could tell where wus hid. (237)

Earlier in the book, Black Ulysses tells the story of Uncles Wailes, a slave who buries the family silver to hide it from the Yankees, and then returns as a ghost to tell his daughter where it is hidden. The authentic setting of this story is verified by one of Dorson's informants, Katy Pointer, who explains a similar tale by commenting,

At that time of the Rebellion them rich planters buried these treasures and then the heirs got to living away, and the houses fell to rock and ruin. When the northern armies was coming, you see, they'd take possession of the plantations, kill the stock and cattle, just take everything. So the planters buried their money and their solid silver. (133)

One story in *Cold Blue Moon* that begins with the motif of the test of staying in the haunted house describes a man and woman who decide to try the test and are visited by a ghost with a beard (H1411). They realize he is a ghost because

this man was growing larger and larger so he kep' this up until he had reach top of the ceiling and his beard wus 'way on the floor by this time. So the lady she spoke to him. She said, "Whut have we did to you in the name of the Lord for you to interfere with us?"

And then he spoke to her. He said, "It is good you spoke when you did. Come and follow me." (238)

The story continues with the ghost revealing two locations where treasure is buried, and after enjoining the woman to give half the money to his son, he disappears.

A subsequent story describes a woman who moves into an old cabin and is visited by a white rooster. She speaks to him, asking, "What in the name of the Lord do you want here?" and then he reveals the site of the buried treasure (239–41). Both these tales contain documented folk motifs, including "Ghost laid when living man speaks to it"

(E451.4), "Ghost laid when treasure is unearthed" (E451.5), and "Ghost responds when spoken to in the name of God" (E391, new number suggested by Roberts [Roberts 281]). Roberts also cites a similar tale in which the ghost helps a woman dig up a buried chest and gives it to her "because she was the only person that had never been afraid of him" (41).

*Cold Blue Moon* also contains several Marster and John tales that have variants in Dorson's collection. Black Ulysses describes one of the Old Colonel's slaves, Old Eli, who "would pray for God to come and get him" every night at nine o'clock. The Old Colonel's son, Marse James, dresses up in a white sheet and visits Eli during his prayers, telling his wife Aunt Jennie, "It is God come to take Eli back with Him out of this hard world" (60). Aunt Jennie answers:

> "Eli is not here, God."
> So God said, "Well, Jennie, I'll have to take you back then." About this time Old Aunt Jennie said, "Eli, you come out from under that bed, you hear God."
> So Eli said, "Well, God, wait and let me get my pants."
> So God said to Eli, "You don't need no pants, I have white robe for you, Eli."
> So Aunt Jennie says, "That sholy is God."
> So Eli said, "Well, God, let me get my hat"; and God said, "Eli, you won't need no hat, I have golden crown for you."
> Old Eli say, "Oh, Lawd, that sholy is Him."
> So Eli said, "Well, God, give me time to get my old shoes."
> So God said, "Come on, Eli, 'cause I have golden slippers for you."
> So Old Eli told Aunt Jennie to open the door. So he looks out and seen Young Marster in white robe. So he says, "Stand back, God, I am comin'." (60–61)

Then Eli runs away. A similar story is told about Uncle Ned, who answers, when God comes to get him: "Well, God, you'll have to come back again, the old man's not in now and best of my recollection he have been dead over fohty years" (63).

One of Dorson's informants, J. D. Suggs, tells a similar story about a slave named Efan who prays for God to take him to heaven. His Marster overhears and goes to Efan's door wrapped in a sheet. His wife Dinah answers the door and says,

> "Efan ain't here." "Well, Dinah," the Lord tells her, "you'll do just as well." Dinah turns around to Efan: "You'd better come out'n from under that bed; you hadn't oughter told the Lord to come out after you."
>
> Efan went out the back door. Old Marster heard him go out and he tuck out after him. Dinah said, "Lord, you just wants to quit. You can't catch Efan, 'cause he's barefooted." (61)

*Cold Blue Moon* contains several other Marster and John tales. One recounts the slave Job's reputation of always being one step ahead of his master. The master decides to

> have some fun with him. So the Old Marster got coon and put him in box. So he calls Job and says unless he tells him what's in box he's gonna git fohty licks, neither is he gonna have anything to eat for two days. If he tells what's in box gonna give him chicken pie fer dinner.

Job is unable to guess what is in the box and finally admits: "Marster, guess coon been runnin' mighty long time, but you got him at last," and Black Ulysses concludes: "He wus signifyin' that Marster caught him in trick, but Old Marster and folks thought he knowed coon was in there. So he got off that time" (128–29).

Dorson cites a variant of the same story, but the Marster has a different motive for testing his slave; he has a bet on Jack's ability to know everything. The tale concludes:

> And then Jack started scratching his head and trying to tell them what was in the box, although he didn't really know. So Carter asked him again, "Well, Jack, what do you say is in the box?" Jack started repeating what Carter had said. He says, "In the box, in the box, in the box." And he decided he didn't know in his mind what, so he just scratched his head and said, "You got the old coon at last." (He was using that as an expression.)

So Old Boss grabbed him and shook his hand and said "Thanks, Jack, thanks, that's just what it is, a coon in them boxes!" (53)

Another Marster and John tale is found in *Cold Blue Moon.* Job stows away on the ship that is carrying his master to Ireland and convinces everyone that he has been swimming the whole way. The master bets with an Irishman that Job can outswim him, so

> Job tells his Old Marster to cook him up sack flour and side o' meat. Irishman asks him whut he wants with it. So old Job tells him he gwine eat it while he's swimmin'. Say sack o' flour and side o' meat last 'im maybe 'bout two weeks and he hopes to git across where he can git somethin' to eat by that time. So Irishman say, "Chris-a-mighty, ain't gonna swim with nobody swimmin' two weeks." And so old Job gets off that time. (131)

Dorson's version of the tale contains the same motifs; the slave convincing the master that he has been swimming across the Atlantic and the master making a bet. The tale concludes:

> The day of the contest he [the challenger] was waiting on the beach, until finally the colored man came, puffing and making a lot of noise, with a cookstove and provisions on his back. He said "Where's that white fellow who's goin' to swim with me?" (in a big voice). The white man said, "Here I am" (in a little voice). John said, "Man, ain't you carrying nothing to eat with you?" He answered "No." "Well, you'd better, for I'm a-fixing to stay." The white man ran away. (55)

It seems clear then, from Odum's use in the trilogy of several folktale types that have parallels in modern folklore collections, that he must have used some authentic material in the books based on his collecting from Left Wing Gordon and possibly other black informants. The most notable omission of black folklore from Odum's trilogy is the absence of animal tales. Fenton notes in her thesis that for many years Joel Chandler Harris influenced the collecting of black tales because most people assumed that the only tales blacks told were animal tales. Odum certainly knew of animal tales, and in *Cold Blue Moon* Black

Ulysses says, "'Bout thousand old songs 'bout animals. I disremembers most of 'em. Animal songs wus befo' days of Blues" (171). This comment suggests that Odum omitted animal tales as well as animal songs from his trilogy because he felt they were associated with the days of slavery and that the blues were more representative of the repertoire and feelings of the modern black person.

As well as including authentic folk material in his trilogy, Odum was also faithful to the performance contexts of black folklore. In her thesis, Joan Fenton discusses a common setting for tale-telling, the lying session. One of her informants "described how in his youth the young men would often swap lies, trying to outdo one another" (34). Fenton finds this description of lying sessions consistent with those described by Zora Neale Hurston, who writes in *Mules and Men* that "it was the habit of the men folks particularly to gather on the store porch of evenings and swap stories" (2). Odum describes a similar scene in *Rainbow Round My Shoulder:*

> Camp scenes again. Noon hour. Other scenes and times. Saturday afternoon or evening or Sunday morning or afternoon. Black men sprawling and resting. Eating finished. Some sleeping, some smoking, some silent. Others talking and bantering and laughing. Black story-tellers improvising tales. Joree jaw and ribald banter. Much laughter and competitive superlatives. (196)

His opening is followed by a series of signifying jokes and then several competing versions of "The Wonderful Hunt."

The stories in *Cold Blue Moon* are framed by a lying session. Odum opens the book with a description of "a gang of Negro laborers seated on old boxes, broken machinery, or sprawling prone on ground or straw . . . and the telling of tales a pastime for artistic story-tellers, run in from work" by a rainstorm (16–17). In their midst is Black Ulysses, who listens condescendingly "to the tame tales of his companions" (17). Gordon listens for a while to a series of stories based on the "fear of staying in haunted house" motif, then interrupts to tell them the "outdashionest story anybody ever heard" (35–36), the story of Big House Hall and all its slaves and masters and ghosts.

In Joan Fenton's analysis of the tall tales of Howard Cotton, a black resident of Chatham County, North Carolina, she speculates that one characteristic of black tall-tale tellers may be their emphasis on improvisation rather than memory in storytelling. Fenton compares Cotton's tales with those of John "Frail" Joines, a white Appalachian tale-teller. She notes that "Joines, like most tellers, presents anecdotes about real people, and tells them as true" (48). Cotton tells stories about imaginary characters, and his stories seem to be more a product of his imagination than an exaggeration of real events (50). Also, Joines's tall tales, and those more common among white storytellers, are brief, comic, and told as the truth. Cotton's improvisational technique, on the other hand, involves introducing the story in a believable way but soon moving to the realm of the absurd, where "the listener knows the story is a lie, and the remainder of the tale just continues the lie further, but at great length" (96). Fenton's thesis seems to point to a different standard of excellence between white and black tale-tellers.

Odum's description of Black Ulysses' storytelling expertise supports Fenton's distinction. Gordon's version of the John Henry tale points to his facility in storytelling and, like Howard Cotton, his delight in detail and exaggeration. Gordon's values are also apparent in his version of the tale, which emphasizes food and women as well as John Henry's legendary strength.

Even if Odum copied the words of his black informants by hand when they were telling tales or singing songs, it seems unlikely that he could have copied the entire text of the trilogy verbatim. One source for many of the images in Black Ulysses' speech may therefore have been not the tales of Left Wing Gordon but the folk songs that Odum collected from Gordon and many others. For example, in *Rainbow Round My Shoulder* Ulysses says, "Trouble gonna follow me to my grave" (231). The same sentiment is found in *Negro Workaday Songs* in the verse: "Trouble, trouble, / I believe to my soul / Trouble gonna kill me dead" (40). The image of Jesus as captain of the "Gospel Train" is found in *Wings on My Feet:* "An' I'm gonna live anyhow till I die, an' if I got to die for my Lord, Cap'n Jesus waitin' in the promised land" (17). In the song "Oh, De Gospel Train's A-Comin'" in *Negro Workaday Songs,* the same image is found in the line "Oh, Marse Jesus am de captain" (202). In *Rainbow Round My Shoulder,* Black Ulysses comments "'Bout funniest thing ever happen to me, also one mos' hard times I ever had, was one time I lay down in woods to sleep an' woke up nex' morning covered with snow. Big black man sleepin' under white freezin' snow" (230). This recollection may be Odum's elaboration on the line "Freezin' ground wus my foldin' bed" (*NWS* 46) as well as an ironic comment on Black Ulysses' situation in a white-dominated world. Since Odum collected these songs from black informants, it follows that the images in the trilogy that are based on song texts are also authentic black folk material.

Clearly, then, Odum collected authentic folk material from black informants, with Left Wing Gordon as a primary source. Although he published folklore in a fictional format, his collection of black folk material is no less valuable than that of other collectors of the time such as Hurston and Puckett. In fact, Hurston's folklore work suffers from much of the same criticism as Odum's because neither of them cited their sources and both conflated material and fictionalized contexts for the material in their books. Of course, Puckett posed as a conjurer in order to collect from informants, so his reputation as a folklorist is also uneven. In the final analysis, perhaps we should just be grateful that these early collectors obtained so much valuable material and published it so that we may analyze it now. Odum's contribution to the field of folklore in terms of the amount of work he did is clear. In addition, because the three novels show his increasing understanding of the collaborative nature of folklore collecting and the importance of context in analyzing material, they paint a useful picture of the development of the field of folklore in the early part of the twentieth century.

# CHAPTER FOUR

# Odum's Literary Collaboration with John Wesley Gordon

A comparison of the three novels in Howard Odum's Black Ulysses trilogy shows a marked advance in the liberalizing of his racial views and in his ability to see Left Wing Gordon as a person, not merely a representative of "the Negro." In *Negro Workaday Songs,* Odum concentrated on Gordon as a representative Everyman, and the classical model of the representative man also informs his Black Ulysses trilogy. But in each of the three books, Black Ulysses becomes more of an individual and less of a stereotype as Odum became increasingly capable of discussing the ways racism had affected Ulysses' life. Although Black Ulysses is clearly intended to represent an African American Everyman, Odum's shift from describing the "group" to writing about a unique individual marks an important step in his intellectual revelations about race and his maturity as a folklorist.

## Format of the Novels

Odum infuses traits of a number of literary genres—epic, myth, folktale—into his three novels, but he creates a work that cannot be defined by any one of these categories. Odum's training as a classicist and sociologist, as well as his years of collecting folk material, helped him find value in both classical and folk art. In combining literary conventions from Western traditions and contemporary African American traditions, Odum created his own genre—a feat that itself was a statement about the worthiness of folk material to stand alongside the great Western classics.

Odum makes overt comparisons to Homer's *Odyssey,* the model for his trilogy. He describes his main character as a man who, "for all appearances . . . might have been thinking gloomily of himself as some noble Ulysses, who 'if it had pleased heaven that this poor man had been born a king . . . would gracefully have filled a throne'" (*RRMS* 1). Chapter 5 of *Rainbow Round My Shoulder* is titled "Beginning His Own Odyssey," and Odum emphasizes the universal quality of Black Ulysses, an Everyman, who "starting as no more than an 'average' nomad, reflects a rare cumulative Odyssey" (68). In the chapter on his relationships with women, "One High Yellow an' Two Teasin' Browns," Odum writes that Black Ulysses "encounters no Goddess Minerva to transport him in his struggles and sufferings, . . . no divine Calypso to share with him her immortality. But Scylla and Charybdis on every hand" (139).

Odum finds a difference, however, between the subject of the ancient epic and his modern story of Black Ulysses: "The ancient poet sang of arms and the man in epic story of group conflict. Not so the Negro, who sings unerringly of personal conflict, himself often the hero" (*RRMS* 179). For Odum, Left Wing Gordon represented the African American secular hero whose battles were fought on a daily basis against a repressive society rather than a foreign enemy. As a result of his increasing sympathy for the plight of individual African Americans, however, Odum does not condemn Black Ulysses for his admiration of black "bad men" or for some of the more violent episodes in his life. Rather, he believes that like Odysseus, the archetypal trickster, Black Ulysses "found guidance in his song communication with the spirits of the bad" (179). Odum does not see the bad man as an antisocial hero any more than the western frontiersman was, although he does contrast Roscoe Bill, Lazarus, Dupree, and others with the "noble exponent of sturdy courage and righteous struggle," John Henry (179–80).

Odum's papers in the Southern Historical Collection contain a typed transcript of portions of Walt Whitman's *Leaves of Grass.* Seemingly, Odum took notes on lines he found especially well written or moving; the notes include longer portions of "Song of the Broad-Axe," "Song of the Exposition," "Pioneers! O Pioneers!" and one or two lines from a number of other poems. Whitman, as the primary representative of America's epic tradition, was also a model for Odum's American epic. Although Odum chose to write in prose, often the style of his opening paragraphs for each chapter is Whitmanesque. For example, the opening pages of the first novel read:

> Sunset and the day's work done. Early November in North Carolina. Green pinetops, red dogwood berries, crimson black-gums and brown-red oaks mingled with shapely cedars. . . . A black man emerging pathward into wooded expanse from a red muddied roadway that had seen better days. . . . Hot supper at camp, clearing skies, cool winds, joreeing conversation, smoke of cigarettes, resurging energies and emotions of eventide. Black Ulysses speaking and singing. (*RRMS* 1–3)

Aside from his thorough knowledge of the epic form and his familiarity with Whitman, Odum had other models to choose from in his use of folk material in literature, including local-color writers like Joel Chandler Harris, but he chose a singularly sociological method of incorporating folklore into literature. Hennig Cohen believes that folklore "appears in American literature in two ways: passively or actively, transcriptively or functionally" (240). In *Our Living Traditions* (1968), Cohen describes Joel Chandler Harris's Uncle Remus tales as an example of the transcriptive use of folklore, in which "a writer presents a more or less authentic transcription of genuine folk material possessing considerable literary appeal in its original state" (240). Cohen believes Harris "had no literary pretensions for his Uncle Remus stories but saw himself as recording faithfully folk material that he knew at firsthand" (241).

Cohen describes several possible functional uses of folklore in literature: "to advance the plot, to characterize, to provide structure, and to defend, explain, and raise questions about the nature of society" (243). One example of the functional use of folklore in American literature is in Nathaniel Hawthorne's works based on New England legends, "which he put to use as a way of exploring social and spiritual questions" (245). In "The Celebrated Jumping Frog of Calaveras County,"

Mark Twain uses a jumping contest between two bullfrogs as a way of "stating the values of civilization as opposed to the values of the frontier" (247). William Faulkner "uses a hunting tale in 'The Bear' to present, among other things, the same conflict" (247).

When applying Cohen's theory to Odum's work it becomes apparent that Odum moved from a largely transcriptive use of folklore in *Rainbow Round My Shoulder* to more functional uses of folklore in *Wings on My Feet* and *Cold Blue Moon.* Folklore in the three books also coincides with a less stereotyped portrayal of blacks in each subsequent book. This change in approach seems largely due to Odum's developing friendship with Left Wing Gordon and his increasing understanding of both the hardships and joys of this black man's life. In addition, Odum was gaining new insights into the political climate in the South, which affected his goal of publishing a black epic.

In some of his nonfiction writing, Odum expresses a desire to use folklore functionally in literature in order to provide some comment on social situations in the South. His "Tentative Memorandum: Regional and Folk Portraiture as Materials for Social Science" describes the importance of works that reflect "the descriptive aspects of social research," particularly those "studies of folk culture which emphasize primarily the more primitive and elementary elements of society" (Odum Papers 1–2). These studies should "throw light upon social capacities, racial capacities, the development of culture patterns and areas" (2). Odum includes his own books *Rainbow Round My Shoulder* and *Wings on My Feet* as among these important descriptive folk-culture studies, so he clearly intended that his trilogy should give his readers a picture of some of "the more primitive and elementary elements of society." However, as Odum continued to work on the books, his attitude toward the "primitive" became much more admiring.

### *Rainbow Round My Shoulder*

In *Rainbow Round My Shoulder,* Odum's portrait of Southern black society emerges largely through the transcriptive use of folklore. Here, tales, songs, and beliefs are bound together by a narrative that is based on the life story of Left Wing Gordon. The book contains little explicit or implicit social comment by the author. Odum took some literary liberties with the material of course; the book is not pure transcription by any means, but the only functional use of folklore in this novel is the use of songs (particularly blues songs) and tales (mostly tall tales) to characterize Black Ulysses.

In this first folk novel, Odum introduces each chapter with an impressionistic description of the scene written in Standard English; the remainder of each chapter consists of stories and songs in black dialect. For example, in the chapter "Remembering First Things," Black Ulysses sings songs about mothers and fathers; songs of love and jealousy are the focus of the chapter "One High Yellow an' Two Teasin' Browns," and the chapters "Don't You Two-Time Me" and "Blues on My Mind" contain several of Black Ulysses' favorite blues songs.

Odum begins his description of Black Ulysses in *Rainbow Round My Shoulder* by depicting him as an artist, first and foremost. In the first chapter, titled "A Twelve-String Laura in the Rough," he describes Black Ulysses' expertise with the guitar before he lost his arm in an accident. Ulysses says,

> This ole 12-string Laura sho' has been in the rough, but she stand by me when my mind's all troubled like water in the deep blue sea. . . . Seems like when I gits to goin' good, pickin' out my tunes and singin', make me forgit eve'ything, ain't no time, ain't no troubles, ain't nothin' but myself an' my feelin's. (3)

Discussing the place of music in his life, Ulysses explains: "'Long with work or travelin', I plays my box an' sings my Blues an' gits folks to help me out when I need 'em, mo' specially good-lookin' womens" (9). According to Odum, "Black Ulysses IS the Blues": he is the oral predecessor of Langston Hughes (251–52).

Black Ulysses' tales and songs reflect his variety of experience. He grew up in a small Southern town with an alcoholic father who beat his wife. She finally shot him in self-defense, and the family went to live with her parents. Ulysses' grandparents taught him much of what he knew about music and storytelling. He idolizes his mother, who was acquitted of killing her husband:

> Mighty hard fer her to have to work out for white folks an' make livin' in daytime, take keer us chilluns an' then come home an' quarrel an' fight with the ole man. Time come when she couldn't stan' it no longer, an' law sho' was right sidin' wid her. (22)

Black Ulysses left school before he was twelve and spent much of his life taking his father's advice: "Don't git crazy on no job—quit, no use stayin' on one thing if you can't git best of it" (28). Odum generalizes from Black Ulysses' experiences and concludes, "The story of Negro childhood and youth in the South" is one of "early disorganization and nomadic trends" (67). Black Ulysses voices the feelings and aspirations of the black bluesman when he says,

> Reasons I travels is can't be satisfied. . . . Sometimes I goes jes' because I likes it. . . . Sometimes I jes' wants to make money. Sometimes I dreams big schemes figgerin' out some big things I'm gonna do. If my good spirit rulin' me, I'm thinkin' 'bout how I can better myself, an' if I feel my hell a-risin' I jes' want to git out o' here. Sometimes I thinks, well, I'm down an' out now, but if I ever gits to end of my journey an' succeed, folks won't know me when I git back. (229)

Some scholars of African American culture have seen two culture groups within overall black culture, the religious and the secular. The bluesman is the prime representative of the secular group, and Left Wing Gordon clearly falls into this category of cultural values and behavior. Blues singers are often fringe members of the local black community—itinerant workers, drinkers and carousers, night people—types of people we often associate with the artistic temperament. Two aspects of this temperament are an inability to be contented with the work and social aspects of everyday life and a desire to break free of social conventions.

A number of the chapters in *Rainbow Round My Shoulder* describe the wandering lifestyle that Odum seems to believe is the source of Left Wing's artistry. In chapter 6 Black Ulysses tells of his youthful exploits in breaking up dances and religious camp meetings. His story is interspersed with songs, including the shout, "I feel it, sister, yes, brother" and the mildly lascivious comment, "Well, sisters used to say sanctified bretherin mighty vigorous feelers when the spirit moved 'em, an' I guess they was" (86).

Odum introduces chapter 7, "Reason I Stay on Job So Long" with the statistic that black workers average "a job a month" (98). Black Ulysses brings life to this number, however, in his descriptions of his early working life. With a sick wife, a child, and no money, he explains, "I couldn't git much of job round home but took whut I could git" (103), including running moonshine and working at dairy and truck farms. The best-paying jobs are at timber and logging "work camps" though, where he encounters a number of tough black men and occasionally a sympathetic white boss: "Mr. Haplane in camp; was jes' fine man as I ever seen anywhere. He would call you by yo' name. . . . If I needed any money he would loan it to me" (118–19).

The one exception to Odum's transcriptive use of folklore in *Rainbow Round My Shoulder* is in chapter 8, where Odum uses Black Ulysses' songs and narrative to "raise questions about the nature of society," in this case, the nature of black work camps. Black Ulysses describes the white contractor Billy Bob Russell, who "had graveyard o' his own" and operated on the premise "Kill a mule, buy another, / Kill a nigger, hire another" (110, 112). The chapter contains descriptions of Black Ulysses' jobs working for white men, many of whom elicit the feelings expressed in one of his songs: "If I had my weight in lime, / I'd whip my captain till I went stone blind" (118).

Along with the hardworking life of an itinerant bluesman, Black Ulysses describes hard play. In "Gambling for My Honey" (chapter 9), he offers a poetic meditation on camp life:

Camp life mighty hard on us boys, an' boys ain't scarcely civilized. Do mos' anything. Still have to have good time an' we forgets it all when we gits plenty of liquor. Like I say, we gits rough an' ready, but got to have it. Got to work, got to fight. (128)

Along with drink, of course, come women and fighting. Black Ulysses is both proud and ashamed of his tricks: "I likely put up with some woman an' make her love me an' maybe I give her fifteen dollars. . . . Then maybe she have saved up a hundred dollars. So I borrows that an' tells her I'll go down to nex' camp an' win with her money. But I don't never come back" (184). His philosophy on fighting is equally practical: "Mos' generally man don't need to shoot nobody or cut 'em up if folks know he mean what he say" (189). Odum calls Gordon "a veteran two-timer moving on to new places" (*RRMS* 153), a description that echoes the stereotypical view of black sexual infidelity found in the folk-song collections.

But if Black Ulysses' attitude toward women is careless, his attitude toward white people is often defiant, and Odum seems to have no qualms about letting whites read what one black man thinks of them. In chapter 21 Black Ulysses says in somewhat Uncle Tomish fashion that he "mos' generally . . . tries to please white folks when I can," but he adds, "when I gits blues an' can't be satisfied . . . I gits in outdashiones' mind, an' cusses white man an' eve'ybody else" (302). Likewise, he says, "I'm gonna work for white folks 'cause that's my duty, leastwise that's onliest way to git 'long," but "ain't gonna ketch me settin' down dyin' for no white man" (303).

Still, he has had cause to thank some whites: "One time mob o' folks caught me an' 'bout to string me up 'cause I look like feller they was huntin'. White man come 'long again an' save me" (306). Odum chooses this chapter to add his own meditation on the difficulties of the race question in the South, but phrased in terms of an individual's story:

Though he travel the world over, to the white man he is a Negro or a number. A part of all that he had met, yet apart from it [an interesting re-working of a line from Tennyson's poem "Ulysses"]. Builder of roads and cities, dependent upon the white man, the white man dependent upon him—work and pay, community and justice, opportunity and outlook. The old Southern order, now no more. The new Southern order, of great variation. . . . New opportunities and new disappointments. . . . How about it, Black Ulysses? How have you fared? What is your verdict? (299–300)

Black Ulysses' song at the end of chapter 21 both gives the chapter a title and answers Odum's opening question:

Oh, Lord, white man, what have I done?
Well, it ain't no use to worry,
An' it ain't no use to whine,
But when you think I'm laughin',
Laughin' to keep from cryin'. (311)

Black Ulysses' story in *Rainbow Round My Shoulder* closes with a sentiment that echoes in the other novels; he says, "I ain't gonna be no black leaf blowed about by white man's breath in some dam' fence corner. I'm gonna blow myself" (304). Despite this defiant note, quoted directly from an African American informant (albeit a fictionalized one), Odum's book was surprisingly well received by white readers and reviewers. Seemingly Odum was correct in his estimation that white readers would enjoy the songs while ignoring the black man's clear sense of self-worth and his anger toward whites.

Despite his willingness to represent justifiable anger in a black character in this novel, Odum still occasionally falls into the trap of attributing the problems of Southern blacks to their own deficiencies in character. In chapter 2 Odum shows a biased view of the "Town and Village Homes of the Southern Negro," people who often have "shiftlessness and undisciplined wastefulness in the chief modes of life. Broken homes and family disorganization, open strife and struggle, wasted energies and resources in men, women and children" (17). Such statements, which are not softened by any comment on the contribution of whites to deplorable scenes in black homes, are reminiscent of the tone of Odum's first book, *Social and Mental Traits of the Negro*.

In light of Odum's professed humanitarian purpose for his trilogy, the stereotypical portrait of Southern blacks that emerged from *Rainbow Round My Shoulder* is surprising. Reviewers of the time typically failed to see the contradictions in Odum's presentation of Black Ulysses' character or his ambivalence regarding racial issues. Biographer Wayne Brazil comments, "Because so much about Ulysses conformed to Southern whites' stereotypes of Negroes, and because 'nature' seemed to account for his basic traits, Odum's presentation of his story did not encourage white readers to examine environmental sources of the black's behavior or to locate blame for his condition in themselves" (575).

The need for such explicit condemnation is evident from contemporary reviews of the trilogy because the books obviously did not threaten whites' complacency about the situation of blacks in the South. In a review of *Rainbow Round My Shoulder* in *The Nation,* Mark Van Doren acknowledges Gordon as the source of the material by noting that "Left Wing is the hero, of course; he has done all the things, he tells all the stories, he sings all the songs" (351). However, Van Doren gives Odum credit for discovering and "transcribing" Gordon's tales and songs, and particularly recommends the book to

> those white people who think they understand the Negro. Understand this energy, this shiftlessness, this sublime indifference to "virtue"? Understand this man who has his own code—perhaps—but knows nothing of the loyalties, supposed to be current and everywhere binding? . . . It will be a chastening experience, one sure to awaken any reader to the still incredible variety, and wildness of our world. (March 28, 1928, 351)

Mary Austin writes in her review of *Rainbow Round My Shoulder* that "the saga of black Ulysses is as patternless as the history of the Negro race in America" and that "*Rainbow Round My Shoulder* must rank with such authentic pieces of American folklore as Uncle Remus, Crashing Thunder, and The Gettysburg Address" (*Saturday Review of Literature,* April 21, 1928, 778–79). Odum was surely highly complimented by this comparison to Lincoln.

H. L. Mencken, an avid reader of *Social Forces* and a fan of Odum's sociological work, also reacted positively to *Rainbow Round My Shoulder* in a review in *American Mercury* (September 1928): "This is one of the most charming documents that I have ever encountered. . . . For the first time the low-down coon of the South—not the gaudy Aframerican intellectual of Harlem and the universities, but the low-down, no-account, dirty and thieving but infinitely rakish and picturesque coon— has found his poet. It is a curious irony that the poet is a white man, a college professor—and a Georgian!" (612–13). Mencken went on to publish two stories in *American Mercury* that eventually became part of Odum's novel *Wings on My Feet,* "Black Ulysses Goes to War" and "Black Ulysses in Camp."

Among contemporary reviewers, only M. P. Levy in *The New Republic* criticizes both Odum's style and the racism in the books. Levy finds Odum's interludes, the prose introductions to each chapter that are written in Standard English

the more significant and less successful part of the book. Less successful, because they interpret the narrative from an intellectual and moral distance; and more significant, because they reflect the distance between the true, masculine labor type and his even most liberal and sympathetic but cloistered friend. The comments are from a distance, kindly but pitying. And Black Ulysses needs no pity. . . . Professor Odum, I think, misses the pertinent fact that each of us provides his own norm, modeled after himself. (September 26, 1928, 159)

Levy is obviously aware of both Odum's racism and his classism, and he finds *Rainbow Round My Shoulder* a proletarian rather than a racial work. "The financial amorality that it reflects, the varied and easy sex life, the brutality—even the habit of song—are the outgrowth rather of the habits of itinerant labor than of negroid inheritance," he writes (159).

Although Levy's criticisms are quite fair, Odum might have felt justified in his largely transcriptive rather than functional use of folklore in *Rainbow Round My Shoulder*—despite its unfortunate outcome of reinforcing, or at least not questioning, stereotypical views of blacks—because of a desire to establish some popularity among readers before becoming more explicit in his social commentary. Although Odum may not have been completely aware of his own racism, he certainly understood the usual racial views of his readers; thus, he may have consciously chosen to write "popular" fiction. Odum's well-known political sensitivity justifies this interpretation, and so does his comment in "Black Rainbow, Random Notes on MS for *Wings on My Feet*" that the books are "not just a Negro story but an American story of human experience. An interesting story and not just another war story. Emphasis upon camps in America important . . . won't satisfy either the extremes of white or Negro" (2). The statement shows a change in the focus of his fiction and an increasing desire to use folk material to raise questions about racial problems in American society. Odum's developing sense of racial injustice in America is clear in the greater incidence of the active or functional use of folklore for social comment in his second novel, *Wings on My Feet*.

Odum was also quite aware of potential reactions to *Rainbow Round My Shoulder* from the African American reading public. His increasing sensitivity is evident in a letter he wrote to Cecile Phillips at Bobbs-Merrill concerning the illustrations for the book. He expresses concern that "any caricature or stage Negro would not only miss the spirit of the book but would offend a great many Negro readers" (December 5, 1927).

Odum also asked his colleague, the prominent African American sociologist Charles S. Johnson, to read the manuscript and comment. Johnson's response in a letter dated January 4, 1928, contains both compliments and corrections. "If it is accepted as the old time sociology of the Negro," he writes, "it will meet objections from Negroes for throwing into relief the least desirable traits of the race, et cetera. If it is accepted as a story of an heroic character whose life was a drama illuminating the field around him it will be a tremendous success. I am inclined to regard it as the latter" (1). Johnson offers some criticisms of Odum's accuracy in reproducing dialect and folk speech: "I pick out sentences like this one: 'Well, ole bitch, I am not going to give you any more of my money,' p. 121. The salutation is Ulysses, but the rest of the sentence is yours, it seems. And it is at such points thru the text that I am inclined to suggest alterations. If you understand what I mean: when the two language levels are mixed the spell breaks" (1). He goes on to point out that "the language of Ulysses is too naïve, sometimes, to portray him as the clever person he must have been" (2). Johnson concludes by noting that Odum, while taking "advanced ground" in portraying Black Ulysses as a "heroic type whose story is fascinating because it represents, not simply racial circumstances, but a restless, adventurous life into which all of the major experiences are crowded," omits the important step of "relating . . . his life to some social purpose different from that which he was supposed to have" (2). Still, Johnson admits, "this would have been sociology, and perhaps, propaganda" (2).

It seems likely that Odum took some of Johnson's criticisms to heart when writing the second book in the Black Ulysses trilogy, because he resolves many of the problems with the incongruity of language and addresses several social issues in greater depth. But there is evidence that Odum also treasured a response to his novel from a working-class African American. Among Odum's papers is a letter from a U.S. Customs officer who found an anonymous typed note in a copy of *Rainbow Round My Shoulder*. In the note, the writer addresses the issue of whether the book should be classified as "fiction, a book of travel, or an autobiography," and the customs officer asks Odum for a response. It is unclear whether Odum ever answered this query, but the question probably interested him enough to keep the letter and the note. The most important aspect of the note for Odum, however, was probably the description of the "Negro janitor" at one bookstore, a "Mr. Andrews" who found the book to be "a true description of the wandering Negro laborer of the South of twenty-five years ago and who is fast disappearing" (November 8, 1929).

Why did Odum write *Rainbow Round My Shoulder*? Was it merely a fictional vehicle for transcription of folk material? Did Odum have literary aspirations? Or did he have some other purpose for writing? The evolution of Odum's other publications of black folk material indicate that he viewed the real Gordon and the fictional Black Ulysses as heroic figures in contrast to the prevailing Uncle Remus, Uncle Tom stereotype. It is significant that he chose a *working man* as his hero, particularly in light of the folk-song publications with Johnson and Johnson's own study of the working hero John Henry. Odum's reasons for choosing Gordon as his folk hero, rather than a better-known black man, might have been artistic; Gordon fit the role of the black Everyman better than more famous black men whom Odum admired, such as Booker T. Washington. But Gordon's experiences as a manual laborer in the South and as a foot soldier in World War I were also more appropriate to Odum's ultimate purpose in writing the trilogy, that of exposing the inhumane living and working conditions of many blacks. In writing the subsequent novels in the trilogy, he continued his exploration of the black psyche and his call for social change.

## Wings on My Feet

*Wings on My Feet,* the novel that focuses on Black Ulysses' experiences in World War I, emphasizes the defiant quality of Ulysses' personality. The general prejudice of whites toward blacks appears in the narrative, songs, and stories of this novel, which is told entirely in Black Ulysses' own words. The book is arranged chronologically rather than thematically, and, again, folk songs provide chapter titles, for example: "Do You Think I'll Make a Soldier?", "Gonna Whet My Blade on Kaiser's Hide," "Me and War Same Thing," and "Ain't Gonna Study War No Mo'." Black Ulysses describes his adventures in boot camp, on the boat going over to France, in battle, and his reception when he returns home to America.

This second book of Odum's trilogy expands the picture of Black Ulysses to expose his survival abilities, his antisocial side, and a compassionate side to his character as well. In true epic-hero fashion, Black Ulysses does not grow and change throughout the course of the trilogy;

his character is essentially the same at thirteen and at thirty-two, but that character is revealed more fully in each subsequent book.

Black Ulysses' defiance is apparent in the opening passage of the book where he describes war:

> War an' me is buddies, fightin's my middle name. What you see in the
> books an' papers I can tell you 'bout an' mo', 'cause I was there. . . .
> Lawd, stayin' there too. I'm magic black boy, rainbow round my shoul-
> der, wings on my feet. War never got me, never will. . . . Me an' war
> same thing. Want me to fight; I been doin' it all my life. (13)

Ulysses makes it clear that work in the Army is nothing compared to the hard physical labor he has performed all his life. He notes how well many other blacks could work and fight, and he has some sym-pathy for "white buddies" who are not accustomed to such hard labor (45, 47).

In this novel we learn about Black Ulysses' lawlessness, particularly in one instance where he attempts murder. He describes his friend from boot camp, Hoof, who was killed over a woman:

> Some black devil slacker bound to git po' Hoof, gonna lay his body
> down. Played bad on him. Must 'a' sneaked up from behind an' shot him
> down. Onliest way could git him. So found him with hole in his
> head 'bout risin' of sun. Said I wus gonna git dam' scoundrel shot po'
> Hoof. (141)

When Black Ulysses sees Hoof's girlfriend with a preacher who says "Hoof wus sinner-man gone to judgment day" (142), he gets the "crazy blues" and "chain-gang blues" (143). He almost succeeds in killing the preacher before the military police interfere. Black Ulysses seems to feel no guilt about this attempted murder; in fact, he swears he will find and kill that preacher one day. He also attributes many instances when he feels his "hell a-risin'" (143) to his anger over Hoof's death.

Although we might interpret Ulysses' actions here as vengeful and foolish, Odum's point was probably a more sympathetic one, that Black Ulysses, as a natural man, believed he could enact justice on his friend's murderer. This interpretation fits both Odum's bias toward a view of black people as creatures of nature without a developed character or social conscience, and his socialist/regionalist agenda of social reforms in the living conditions of blacks so that natural justice would be unnecessary.

For all the supposed "primitive" aspects of Black Ulysses' personality, he is a good judge of character, and his exposure to different types of people in the war gives him ample subjects for study. He describes the men on board the ship returning home as "some quality white folks on board, some po' white trash. Some finest officers anybody ever seen, some mean as hell I know. . . . Some fine colored boys, some jes' natchelly too turrible to live" (281).

He also has a healthy view of his own character and place in the world:

> Me, I'm quality. . . . I'm white man an' black man, high yellow an' brown, blue-vein angel an' devil saint. . . . I'm Africa an' good old U.S.A. . . . I'm greyhound outrunnin' eagle shadow. I'm gorilla breakin' bones of man, I'm fightin' devil an' peaceful saint. . . . I'm hoodoo an' magic, an' I'm King Jesus' bosom friend. (281–84)

Black Ulysses encounters racism even though he is fighting for American freedom. He recalls a time when a "big white man got to cussin' soldiers sayin' Uncle Sam ain't gonna have no dam' black bastards fightin' fer him" and "'nother station white man wus drunk, staggerin' round an' hollerin', yes, by God, Uncle Sam had plenty nigger soldiers to fight war fer him. White boys gonna stay home an' have good time" (162). He describes the lynching of a black soldier in France by white soldiers who claimed he had raped a French girl. Ulysses comments, "Army don't have to fight Jerries, got plenty colored folks to fight" (90).

War makes Black Ulysses think about the way black men are treated in America. He describes a race riot where a "crowd went on out in colored section close to white folks' houses. One old colored man wus crippled an' couldn't git 'way when they told him to leave. Begged white folks not to kill him. Shot him jes' like snake or mad dog or varmint' or sumpin'. . . . Ain't seen no Heines meaner'n that" (88).

Black Ulysses had one positive racial experience in the war, however, when he got to meet African soldiers. He had heard stories about Africans from his grandfather, who had come to America on a slave ship when he was a young boy. Black Ulysses says, "He never seen all things he told us 'bout, but his father told him 'bout 'em" (60). The grandfather told about fierce battles, "Chiefs so terrible make tigers tremble" (60), African soldiers who "would dress up in shinin' colors, and march an' sing an' dance an' fight" (61). He also tells of fighting "side by side with black soldiers from Africa, fightin' with white man 'gainst 'nuther white man" (57), an experience he remembers when he returns to the United States to find that nothing has changed for blacks. He and other black soldiers "thought we gonna be livin' easy, gonna be livin' high" (296), but whites told him he could not wear his uniform. One soldier had his uniform torn off; another disappeared without a trace.

Black soldiers certainly encountered prejudice and discrimination even on the battlefield, but many of them, including Black Ulysses, returned home with a greater sense of their right to participate fully in American society and a greater understanding of their heritage through encounters with other American and African blacks.

*Wings on My Feet* ends on both a hopeful and defiant note. Black Ulysses tells us, "Me an' war same thing. Had it all my days. Gonna have it till I die. Howsomever, war never got me, never will. Got my buddies, never got me" (308).

In this book, Odum uses Black Ulysses' story to comment quite openly on white racial prejudice; unfortunately, the fact that most of Odum's readers were interested in folklore only as entertainment, not as the vehicle for social comment, is apparent from the reception of *Wings on My Feet*. The book did not sell well, and Emmet Kennedy's review in *Southern Review of Literature* seemed to reflect many readers' opinions: "As an authentic, emotional record of the attitude of mind of the American negro soldier during the late war, *Wings on My Feet* contains much that is interesting and diverting" (244). Kennedy and others were seemingly oblivious to the painful social issues raised by the book.

Black Ulysses sums up his assessment of social conditions in America by saying, "White man in South principled up like this, jes' ain't gonna think 'bout colored man as equal" (298). For Odum to have used the word "equal," even in fictional work and spoken by a black character, was quite a step from his "hope that the Negro desired to comprehend the essential weakness of the race," expressed in the introduction to *Social and Mental Traits of the Negro*.

Correspondence between Odum and his publisher, D. L. Chambers at Bobbs-Merrill, however, indicates that Odum became concerned that low sales of *Wings on My Feet* meant he had gone too far. He suggests that Chambers advertise the book by quoting from reviews calling it a "black *All Quiet on the Western Front*" that "belongs in every library of the war" (February 18, 1930). Chambers's reply of April 14, 1930, shows that he realized Odum needed an explanation for the difference in sales between the first two books. "Perhaps the explanation can be found in the fact that the surprise element was to be found in the first book," he wrote. "You were doing something quite distinctly 'different' and the difference was more striking in the first attack. . . . Then too, I think the rhapsodical quality is more emphasized in WINGS than in RAINBOW, and the development of the story is sacrificed, is less obvious." Chambers avoids mentioning another possible explanation for low sales, that *Wings on My Feet,* published only ten years after World War I, was too explicit in describing recent racial injustice in the South.

Although Odum indicated that he wondered whether he should continue writing the third book in the trilogy, it seems unlikely that he was merely concerned about making more money from *Wings on My Feet* (Letter to D. L. Chambers, January 21, 1930). If anything, the publication of the third book in the trilogy would probably have made the entire series more popular. A more plausible explanation for Odum's obvious uneasiness about completing the third book is that he planned to be more open in using folklore as a vehicle for social comment.

## Other World War I Memoirs by African Americans

Although reviewers and readers of the day found *Wings on My Feet* less engaging than Odum's previous book, it is arguably the best of the three novels from a literary standpoint. Odum uses a less intrusive narrative technique in this book: he allows Black Ulysses to speak for himself, with no introductions by a narrator. This book is essentially a black man's memoir of World War I ghostwritten by a white folklorist; as such, it compares favorably with other memoirs written by African Americans about their World War I experiences. In many ways, Odum's novel is the least racist of these memoirs; thus, his book is an important contribution to a more complete understanding of the role of African American soldiers in the war.

Since *Wings on My Feet* is ostensibly a work of fiction, can it honestly be seen as a memoir by an African American? Odum cites Left Wing Gordon as a source in *Negro Workaday Songs,* and in *Cold Blue Moon* Odum directly refers to Gordon as "Black Ulysses, the same old John Wesley Gordon, nicknamed Left Wing Gordon, self-styled alias of 'Wing,' back again from another Odyssey, back at his old job—greatest water boy and helper in America, maybe in the world" (17). In addition to this clear reference to Gordon as the alias of Black Ulysses, the folklore in the trilogy verifies the authenticity of Odum's research with black informants (see chapter 3). Although both *Rainbow Round My Shoulder* and *Cold Blue Moon* show evidence of folk material from other sources—folk songs Odum collected early in his career, folk rhymes and beliefs he may have gotten from Puckett's book, and ghost stories and Marster and John tales he might have learned from Gordon or other informants—it seems likely that Odum based the novels on John Wesley Gordon's life and included a great deal of material from Gordon that he copied verbatim. If Johnson's timetable is correct, Odum learned the John Henry tale from Gordon three years before Johnson wrote *John Henry.* Seemingly, then, Gordon had left Chapel Hill before Odum wrote *Cold Blue Moon,* the least coherent of Odum's novels in terms of plot; the book is loosely unified only by the theme of ghost stories told by Black Ulysses to his fellow workmen. The first two novels, on the other hand, give Black Ulysses' life history, but *Wings on My Feet* is the only novel to tell the story chronologically as in a conventional novel. *Wings on My Feet* is also the only book of the three in which Odum omits introductory sections in Standard English, the portions of the other two books that we would assume represent Odum's personal voice. Black Ulysses tells his own story in his own words in *Wings on My Feet,* and it seems unlikely that Odum would have cobbled together this story of one black man's experience in World War I from several different informants. Logically, then, *Wings on My Feet* is the memoir of an African American soldier dictated to a white folklorist.

*Wings on My Feet* compares favorably with other memoirs from World War I, even those written by African American soldiers, in its lack of racial bias. *Twenty-Two Months with "Uncle Sam": Being the Experiences and Observations of a Negro Student Who Volunteered for Military Service Against the Central Powers from June, 1917 to April, 1919* is a published diary written by John Brother Cade, a professor of history at Paine College in Augusta, Georgia. Cade claims his purpose in writing is to provide a "spark which will ignite a literary conflagration leading to a larger and nobler effort in the historical study of the 92nd and 93rd Divisions" (7). He bemoans "the gross ignorance of the drafted men" who are his fellow black soldiers because "fully ¼ of them could not write their names" (26–27). The author gives a list of songs that were popular among black soldiers and includes some song texts (39–40).

In *Colored Soldiers,* collector W. Irwin MacIntyre claims in the preface that "these stories are given as received by and without recourse upon THE AUTHOR." The author is an educated black man who uses a condescending tone when telling a number of humorous stories: "I was a colored soldier at Camp Gordon. . . . We had many amusing experiences with illiterate and inexperienced members of my race" (37). His narrative focuses on humor at the expense of his fellow black soldiers. In one story, "A Wife's Revenge," he describes how one soldier told his sweetheart to find another because he was not coming back to the States. She replies that she'll just keep the one she had before he left (chapter 14). Another soldier claims, "I dropped a heap er de green endurin' de wah. But I couldn't git shed er de black" (58). In "The Blood Test," MacIntyre explains that John Henry "became a good soldier but what his old mother would have called 'a biggity en stu'k-up nigger'" (60). Henry is impressed by the lack of a color line in Europe and debates whether he should stay in France where the economic situation is bad but his social opportunities are good, "or should he return to the country for which he had so bravely fought and which was sure to recognize his patriotism but not his social standing?" (61). His mother tells him to "git shed er dem biggity ways" (64). In this collection of stories, the author expresses sympathy for the disenfranchised black man, but his tone separates him from his informants.

One of the most complete memoirs of World War I by black writers is the *Complete History of the Colored Soldiers in the World War* (1919), written by two sergeants, two privates, and one corporal. These five men claim that the material in their book is "absolutely true" as it is based on "individual stories, regimental histories, and pictures taken right on the field of battle" (foreword). The book is a quite thorough history; it contains both official and personal letters and a number of first-person descriptions of battles and military life. The first-person accounts are all written in Standard English; there is no use of dialect in the book at all. The authors comment on black soldiers from other countries: Somalia, South Africa, Morocco, and "The Colored Boys from British West Indies" (115–17). The writers obviously intend the book as a testament to contributions of black soldiers to the war, and they end with a criticism of racism, writing that "Race prejudice is pro-Germanism" (153) and "SEGREGATION IS WRONG. IT IS DANGEROUS. . . . THIS GREAT WORLD WAR WILL HAVE BEEN FOUGHT IN VAIN FOR AMERICA IF IT DOES NOT BRING BLACK AMERICA AND WHITE AMERICA CLOSER TOGETHER" (159). This history was certainly a positive contribution to the on-going debate on race issues after the war, but its impact is somewhat weakened by the fact that the authors call themselves and fellow soldiers "boy" throughout the book.

We see a rather stereotypical literary portrayal of a black World War I soldier in the character of Caspey in William Faulkner's *Sartoris.* Faulkner portrays Caspey as lazy and rebellious; he "returned to his native land a total loss, sociologically speaking, with a definite disinclination toward labor, honest or otherwise, and two honorable wounds incurred in a razor-hedged crap game" (62). Caspey tells several of his war adventures to an admiring audience consisting of his father, sister, and nephew; he claims, "I don't take nothin' offen no white man no mo', lootenant ner captain ner M.P. War showed de white folks dey can't git along widout de cullud man. . . . And now de cullud race gwine reap de benefits of de war, and dat soon" (66). His father is not so sure, especially when Caspey elaborates: "And de women, too. I got my white in France, and I'm gwine git it here, too" (66). His father, Simon, responds, "De good Lawd done took keer of you fer a long time, now, but He ain't gwine bother wid you always" (66).

William Faulkner also wrote a story called "The Wishing Tree" for a little girl named Victoria. In this fantasy story, not published until 1964, the little brother of the main character wishes for a soldier. Suddenly, the husband of their maid Alice appears and tells them of his adventures in World War I. Alice's husband complains about traveling "over there" for the war: "A hundred days, and jes' water, up and down and up and down, and when you looked out you never seen nothin'. . . . I knowed they killed folks in wars, but it seemed like day after day that I jes' couldn't die. I don't know how in the world folks ever dammed up a pond that big" (46). "I never seed a soldier yet that ever won anything in a war," he concludes. "But then, whitefolks' wars is always run funny. Next time the whitefolks has a war, I think I ain't goin'. I think I'll jes' stay in the army instead" (48).

Odum's narrative is a refreshing alternative to these largely stereotypical portrayals of African American soldiers in World War I. Unlike many other first-person black accounts of the war, *Wings on My Feet* is not primarily a humorous book but rather a very serious account of Black Ulysses' adventures. He tells occasional funny tales about both blacks' and whites' attempts to get out of army service, but his primary focus is the hard work and brutality of war as well as the inhumane treatment of black soldiers. He describes white military police stringing up a "colored soldier an' fill him full o' bullets" (59) and how whites are crueler than even native African warriors (66). Black Ulysses is reminded of his first race riot in the United States where whites killed an innocent young black man "jes' like kill rabbit" (87). He also remembers an incident on a plantation when over two hundred blacks failed to stand up to one white man (89).

Like Caspey, Black Ulysses refuses to accept unequal treatment as a black soldier. He describes an occasion when a lieutenant fails to treat him "like soldier" and Black Ulysses and his friends throw the man in a boxcar. He explains, "If treat me right, I treats them right; if be pleasant to me, I be pleasant to them; if treat me rough, I'm mean as hell I know" (119–20). He also describes witnessing a black superior officer disciplining a white officer (121–22).

Odum includes graphic details about racism and the horrors of war in Gordon's memoir that other writers omit. For example, Black Ulysses is appalled by Britons who "would pull blouse to see if colored men had tails. Been told wus like monkeys, jes' didn't know better" and he concludes that the "French heap better than that an' treat colored soldier like man" (199–200). He also describes a day after the Armistice when black soldiers were assigned the duty of re-burying improperly buried bodies. Black Ulysses claims that since then "I ain't never gonna eat no mo' salmon long as I live. Make me think 'bout dead bodies dug up" (264).

Odum provides a clear account of Black Ulysses' reception upon his return to the United States; whites tell him to remove his uniform and he "tells 'em I'm soldier of Uncle Sam, I been fightin' in France, can't do nothin' with me" (297). A crowd of white "boys" force him to leave town and he concludes, "Nothin' to do 'bout it. I can do what I have to do, an' maybe time come when I have to do it" (298). Still, meditating on injustices against blacks leads to his life-changing injury. While working on a construction gang after the war, Black Ulysses is thinking about his experiences: "Must 'a' got keerless 'cause 'bout that time stone crusher come down on my arm. . . . So lost my left arm. Nothin' to do about it, goddam" (305).

In the concluding pages of *Wings on My Feet,* Odum illustrates the paradox of Black Ulysses' training as an American soldier and the role he is expected to play in the postwar South. In performing his duties as a night watchman, Black Ulysses tells a hidden intruder to halt, but he is forced to shoot because the man "does not comply with my order" (307). It turns out to be a white man, so Black Ulysses is under guard in the local jail to "keep folks from stringing me up" because "I done whut I wus told to do in army" (307). He explains that some "good white folks got me off" but he "ain't gonna study war no mo' " (308–9).

*Wings on My Feet* is a remarkable achievement when we compare its narrative and tone to that of other World War I memoirs written by black soldiers. Not only does Odum explicitly condemn the treatment of black soldiers by whites, he allows a black man to tell his own story in his own words. This book is also a better novel than the other two books in the trilogy; Odum includes fewer songs and the narrative seems more natural and less of a hodgepodge of songs and stories. Finally, this folk novel provides an important alternative view of the experiences of African American soldiers in World War I.

## Cold Blue Moon

The final book in the trilogy, *Cold Blue Moon,* is a collection of ghost stories and other tales told in dialect. Odum uses folklore functionally in this novel, but by writing about the antebellum plantation system and commenting on racial injustice through the device of folk ghost tales, he distances himself, and his readers, from the material. Odum uses a framing device in this novel, having Black Ulysses tell the stories to his fellow construction workers during a rainstorm. Odum is possibly indebted to Newbell Niles Puckett's book, *Folk Beliefs of the Southern Negro* (1926), for some of the story motifs in this book. Again in this book, Odum sets the scene in each chapter and groups the tales by subject. In "Thundering Down the Stretch," Black Ulysses tells of the Old

Marster's horses; "A Hundred Hounds Belling the Woods" contains hunting tales; and ghost stories provide material for several chapters, including "Cold Blue Moon and Blue-Roan Horse" and "Roll-Call of Ghosts and Roll-Call of Ha'nts."

Black Ulysses tells stories that he purportedly learned from his grandfather about a prosperous antebellum Southern plantation called Big House Hall. As part of a work crew that is sitting out a rainstorm while renovating the old house into a modern hunting and riding club, Black Ulysses tells stories of the plantation's past glory and misery. However, the novel is also a vehicle for Odum's criticisms of the South and slavery.

Black Ulysses tells of the days of glory for Big House Hall, the setting for horse races, fox hunting, and gala entertainments by describing the crops, the food, the land, and the family that owned it all. The Old Colonel was a hard but fair man, his wife was a good and kind woman, and his family and way of life were torn apart by the Civil War.

Some of the reputed ghosts on the old plantation are former slaves who have borne injustices from the Old Colonel's family. His father was a wicked and cruel man; one story describes the ghosts of his slaves killing him by tearing him limb from limb (140–41).

Another story tells about a slave who was the maid of Miss Amy, the Colonel's daughter. She wanted her husband to be with her, but the Colonel wouldn't sell the man to Miss Amy's husband. After the maid stole Miss Amy's baby and accidentally killed it, Miss Amy's ghost has been seen looking for her baby (180–81).

Yet another story tells of a slave who was falsely accused of killing Miss Bella, the fiancée of the Colonel's son, and then lynched. A local tree was reputed to be haunted because "big brown boy wus hung in it by crowd of white men an' boys an' never did take his body down till buzzards come after it" (263).

There is also the story of an elderly black slave, Uncle Wailes, who hid the family silver and was tortured and killed by Yankee soldiers. His ghost came back and led his daughter to the hiding place (204–9). Although the daughter returns the silver to her white mistress, it is significant that it is she, and not a white person, who is led to the hiding place.

Another story tells how the Colonel's son, Marse James, was found dead on the front porch one morning long after the war. He had become a dissolute young man and was supposedly killed by the ghosts of two slaves he murdered for insulting his mother. Black Ulysses comments that James was "always good to slaves. [James] sholy did hate to do it" (197). Either this is a naïve statement for a black man to make about a Southern white slaveholder, or Black Ulysses is being ironic. In any case, poetic justice is obviously satisfied by the story.

Each of these stories places at least some of the blame for the Civil War and subsequent social problems in the South on the white slave-owner. Odum comments on the Civil War and its causes in several chapters of *Cold Blue Moon*. He writes that the South's history goes "a long way from first slow slave ships to the last fast-riding youth" (189). When he describes the "black men at home, put to the test, some faithful beyond measure, some turned traitor to the old cause, advocate of the new" (190), Odum's words reflect the traditional white view that slaves should have been faithful to their masters, an obvious contradiction in terms. But Black Ulysses' view is, interestingly enough, quite similar. He tells of "Yankees comin' nearer an' slaves runnin' off an' stealin' an' actin' biggity. Old slaves powerful disgusted with 'em, but can' do nothin' 'bout it" (197). These may be Odum's rather than Left Wing Gordon's words, or perhaps Gordon is quoting his grandfather. Gordon may also have refrained from expressing his real thoughts to a white folklorist, which would explain his seeming ambivalence in describing his own reaction to such a situation: "Lawd, Lawd, don't know would I run off, neither do I know would I have stayed" (198).

The stories also contribute to one of the themes of the novel, the interrelatedness of all human beings, both black and white. Black Ulysses describes himself both as a "black man sleepin' under white freezin' snow" and as a "white spirit ramblin' under hot black skin" (270). Since there is never any hint in the books that Black Ulysses is of mixed race, this comment seems to underline Odum's belief, or Left Wing

Gordon's belief, that Southern culture, ultimately American culture, is mixed. Odum felt that improving whites' and blacks' understanding of each other's culture was the key to a new South. He comments in this novel on a South "embattled behind religion and race, a South enslaved to tradition and fear" and a North "embattled behind impatience and steel, a North oblivious of how cultures grow" (260). Both the region and the nation, according to Odum, need "knowledge of the past" and "guidance for the future" (261).

Part of that future is seen in Odum's review of African American history and his "roll-call of black men . . . an epic and an epoch in the Western World" (255). They are

> not yet told in story nor written in books. Weave of a nation, fabric of history. Millions turned North, more millions South. Climbing to the high places, working in the low. Doctors and teachers, lawyers and preachers, builders of fortunes, founders of caste. Phi Beta Kappa's and Ph.D.'s, honor men and grid men, writer men and play-boys acting on the stage. White-coated Pullman porters, traveling the country through, seeing the world. Red caps, masters of strategy, artists and workers, college men and common men, dual persons in a white man's world. Writers of the blues, singers of songs. (255–56)

Criticizing the tradition of gentility in the Old South was surely difficult for Odum, but through folklore, particularly ghost tales, he was able to distance himself from the material and more openly comment on "a perfect past which could not endure because of its imperfections" (11). For example, the final story in *Cold Blue Moon* recounts the death of Old Colonel, a man who is hardly the ideal Southern gentleman. His half-black daughter cares for him on his deathbed, and he dies one evening when he sees the ghost of his other daughter, Little Mistis, standing next to her. Black Ulysses comments on the colonel's death with some sympathy, saying he has nothing left "from Big House Hall an' slaves an' quality folks, 'scusin' ghosts an' ha'nts walkin' in light of cold blue moon." But Black Ulysses himself expresses no regret for a cultural system that has affected his own life in such a negative way that he will leave "walkin' an' talkin' to myself an' won't be satisfied here an' nowhere I go" (278).

Odum's technique of distancing himself and his readers from the material was so successful that reviewer Jonathan Daniels could see the book as merely "a lively and poetic anthology of the ghost stories of the American Negro," commenting that "like all Mr. Odum's books about the Southern Negro this volume is not only authentic but rich and vivid as the Negro's own life, sensuous but also full of hilarity, and full of pain" (774). Perceptive modern readers can see, however, that Odum used the folk ghost tales to raise questions about racial injustice in the South, not only on the antebellum plantation but in his own time.

It certainly seems clear that Odum made personal progress over the years in achieving more liberal racial views when we compare his 1910 publication, *Social and Mental Traits of the Negro,* which attempted to provide scientific justification for segregation, to his subsequent folk-novel trilogy, which emphasized the inhumanity of racial injustice. The failure of Odum's readers to achieve similar enlightenment is due either to Odum's inability to be as explicit as he needed to be for his audience or to their own inability to accept Odum's criticisms of the South.

The relationship of the story of Black Ulysses to Odum's social agenda becomes clear in the last chapter of *Rainbow Round My Shoulder.* Odum recognizes that Black Ulysses, at age thirty-two, has completed only one stage of his wanderings, and that Odum's attempt at describing this odyssey must represent only the beginnings of a "more sensitive and creative fiction true to and worthy of the innermost life and character of Black Ulysses and other physical and spiritual adventurers like him" (316). Odum views his own fiction with humility; it is "representative yet of only the observer's art" (316), but he feels attempts at fiction about folk characters like Black Ulysses are important because "in him have met from other days the organic forces and essence of life as eternal as the folk-soul in the making" (316). Odum could not overcome the monumental problem of being a white man telling a black man's story, and he recognized that his was only a first step toward better and more authentic fictional renderings of African

American culture, but he did take that step, and in doing so provided the groundwork for other writers, new views, and his own dream of a New South.

In *Rainbow Round My Shoulder,* Odum expresses his own hopes for his fictional trilogy, that his story of a "Negro wanderer" will "tempt us only to such foolish joys as may enable us to understand better the heritage, vicissitudes and annals of a black man who has traveled farther and longer than Ulysses but who still comes singing" (317).

Clearly, fiction was a good outlet for Odum's ideas because through it he could showcase the folklore that he admired and criticize the South he loved without facing the public disapproval aroused by more "scientific" studies. In his analysis of Odum's trilogy, Daniel Singal concludes that Odum was "placing himself inside Black Ulysses' skin to explore the exotic but forbidden world of black culture," with the result that "Black Ulysses' very survival became a wonderment for Odum, bespeaking the extraordinary folk vitality his *black soul mate* was endowed with" (emphasis mine). Singal also explains that "the element of moral loathing, the fear of contamination that had rendered his previous research [on African Americans] 'nauseous and gruesome' had entirely disappeared," a change Singal explains by citing the acceptance of environmentalism among American intellectuals, an acceptance that freed Odum "from many of his Victorian shackles" (*War Within* 144–46). That changing scientific ideas about race influenced Odum's thought is supported by Guy Johnson, who wrote in Odum's obituary that before his death Odum "welcomed the Supreme Court decision of 17 May 1954 and prepared to write *Agenda for Integration*" ("Howard Washington Odum: An Appreciation" 102). But, more importantly, his relationship with Left Wing changed Odum's views.

It seems certain, in fact, that Odum's change of heart began long before 1954 and was largely due to his work as a folklorist, work that necessitated intimate encounters with an individual black informant, rather than to the more general sociology work he published earlier. A letter to Cecile Phillips at Bobbs-Merrill illustrates this intimacy with Gordon: "There are a great many places in [Left Wing's] life when there is poignancy and sometimes poetry. I have sat beside him, admired his profile, his face with blood vessels standing out and perspiration bursting out and his physical earnestness. While we do not sentimentalize over him, we do treat him as a human being rather than as the mere Negro" (December 5, 1927).

In looking at Odum's folklore work, we can see evidence of a change in attitude and thought brought on by learning methods of study in the fields of sociology and folklore from Guy Johnson and from his friendship with Left Wing Gordon. Singal and other analysts of Southern intellectual history point to Odum's belief in the dispassionate nature of science and his realization, when "the verdict of science came in" at the end of the 1920s, that there was no longer any real scientific basis for the belief that blacks were inferior. But it seems unlikely he would have accepted so willingly "the verdict of science," as many Southern intellectuals of his day did not, without the two intimate friendships that folklore brought him: one with a colleague who had more liberal views, the other with a working-class African American man who eventually came to represent, for Odum, some of the best that human beings were capable of being, a reality for the classical heroes he studied and admired.

CHAPTER FIVE

# Folklore and Racial Tolerance
# in the Academy

aniel J. Singal opens part 2 of his study of Southern intellectual history, *The War Within: From Victorian to Modernist
Thought in the South, 1919–1945,* with a chapter on Howard
Odum. Under the title "Modernists by the Skin of Their Teeth," Singal
groups Odum, Faulkner, and the Agrarians together, describing them
all as writers who were "straddling two cultural eras" and thus had the
"unparalleled opportunity to view the South with fresh eyes, using the
conceptual tools made available by the social sciences and the perspectives afforded by Modernist literary culture in bringing to light facets
of Southern society previously ignored" (111). This straddling position
offered both disadvantages and advantages. On the one hand, "the
work of these writers was marked by a certain tentative quality; never
would they obtain the sure apprehension of their subject enjoyed by
those starting fully Modernist in the mid-1930s." On the other hand,
these figures "also possessed a chance for broad-ranging exploration
far more extensive than their successors" (111).

Singal finds that the hallmark of these men's writing was a "thor-
oughgoing ambivalence," which, in the case of Odum, took the form
of "portraiture," a method of distancing himself from his material by "a
depiction of Southern society that laid bare the pathology and many of
its causes without analyzing or identifying it by name" (112). Odum's
ambivalence, according to Singal, sparked his immense creativity, but
it was only the succeeding generation of Southern modernists who
could build on Odum's work, "facing Southern ills with a measure of
detachment and working steadily to help correct them" because they
"understood that the irrational could never be wholly eliminated from

human existence; that, on the contrary, its presence was often to be desired" (113).

Singal concentrates on Odum's sociological work, but his point applies to Odum's work as a folklorist as well. Odum's folklore work is sometimes flawed by the ambivalence that Singal describes, but it provided inspiration for further folklore studies, particularly at the University of North Carolina. Moreover, the folklore work of truly modernist faculty members at the university became characterized by a greater willingness to investigate and attempt to solve Southern problems.

The folkways of North Carolina seemed both unique and perishable to many of Odum's colleagues at the University of North Carolina, and his work gave both inspiration and prestige to the studies of members of the university intellectual community who wanted either to record or change traditional ways of life. Odum's treatment of folk studies as empirical investigations provided a scientific basis for the interest in folklore among many members of the faculty. He provided practical support for folklore work to members of the IRSS, and he supported publication of their work in the *Journal of Social Forces* and by the University of North Carolina Press. Also, Odum was an important contributor to the overall intellectual milieu at the University of North Carolina. Along with such colleagues as William Terry Couch, editor of the UNC Press, and Frederick Koch, founder of the Carolina Playmakers, Odum helped establish the University of North Carolina's reputation as a pioneering institution in the field of folk studies. Finally, Odum gave personal inspiration and encouragement to younger faculty members, particularly fellow sociologist Guy B. Johnson and playwright Paul Green. In fact, these younger friends of Odum absorbed his ideals and in some ways transcended the work of their mentor, Johnson in the field of folklore/sociology research with the publications of *John Henry* (1929) and *Folk Culture on St. Helena Island* (1930), and Green in his use of folklore as the basis for social themes in his folk plays.

## Odum and the UNC Press

According to Singal and others, Odum, as director of the Institute for Research in Social Science, was an important figure in establishing the reputation of the University of North Carolina Press as a major university publishing house. Singal writes that "the heart of the press's publishing schedule . . . the work that brought it the most public notice and drew the greatest critical fire, consisted of the regional social science studies it brought out on behalf of Odum's institute" (276). He cites several titles, among them Arthur F. Raper's *The Tragedy of Lynching* (1933), Roy M. Brown's *Public Poor Relief in North Carolina* (1928), Jennings J. Rhyne's *Some Southern Cotton Mill Workers and Their Villages* (1930), and Wiley B. Sanders's *Negro Child Welfare in North Carolina* (1933), as some of the volumes published by the university press that "clearly dealt with subjects Southerners had not been accustomed to discussing" (276).

Louis Wilson claims that Odum was responsible for an important university press policy change; Odum convinced the board that it should accept manuscripts from outside the university community (Wilson 492). Wayne Brazil comments that "the Press gained considerable recognition as the initial publisher of *The Journal of Social Forces,* but the decisive event in its history was the founding of the Institute" (546). However, Brazil notes that Odum and the press "were at odds frequently during the late 1920s and early 1930s over the quality of Institute manuscripts. Odum was so intolerant of criticism that the Press eventually agreed to allow the Institute staff to do all the editing and proof reading of Institute manuscripts" (549).

This policy caused some problems for UNC Press editor W. T. Couch, who often felt that Odum and other members of the university press board of governors were too conservative. He sometimes managed to outmaneuver them, however, as he did when the press published E. C. L. Adams's *Congaree Sketches* (1927). Odum and the other members of the board of governors did not object to Adams's book but to the introduction, which, at Adams's request, had been written by Paul Green. In the introduction, Green observes that "black and white are inextricably mingled in blood and bone and intention" and that it is whites' obligation to extend a helping hand to blacks (x). The board agreed to destroy all copies of the book and reprint it without the introduction, until Couch informed them that "more than a hundred advance copies of *Congaree Sketches* had already been distributed to reviewers, leading literary figures, and major bookstores throughout the country" (Singal 267). The board decided to go ahead with the publication of the book and learned something in the process, because, as Singal notes, "The Klan did not march on Chapel Hill, the legislature did not vindictively cut the university's budget, nor did the press, despite the book's heavy sales in the South, receive so much as one protest letter" (267).

Odum and the press board may have disagreed with Couch, Paul Green, and other young liberal scholars about potential political ramifications from publishing controversial texts, but the University of North Carolina Press did publish quite a few folklore manuscripts at Odum's suggestion. Not only did the press publish Odum and Johnson's two folk-song studies, *The Negro and His Songs* and *Negro Workaday Songs,* as well as Johnson's two independent folklore books, *John Henry: Tracking Down a Negro Legend* and *Folk Culture on St. Helena Island,* it also published T. J. Woofter's St. Helena Island study, *Black Yeomanry* (1930), and other folklore manuscripts. Odum recommended two books on black folklore by writers who were not members of the institute, and these were also published by the press: *Folk Beliefs of the Southern Negro* (1926), by Newbell Niles Puckett, and *The Negro Sings a New Heaven and a New Earth* (1930), by Mary A. Grissom. Other books listed under the topic of folklore in *Books from Chapel Hill: A Complete Catalogue, 1923–1945* (1946) include tales collected by James R. Aswell and others of the Tennessee Writers' Project under the title *God Bless the Devil!* (1940); Martha Warren Beckwith's *Black Roadways: A Study of Jamaican Folk Life* (1929); *Old Songs and Singing Games* (1938), collected by Richard Chase; *Haiti Singing* (1939), by Harold Courlander; and George Pullen Jackson's *White Spirituals in the Southern Uplands* (1933). The University of

North Carolina Press also published the journal Odum founded, *The Journal of Social Forces,* which often included reviews of these and other folklore books.

## Odum's Influence on Guy Johnson

Earlier in this book, I discuss the important influence of Guy B. Johnson's liberal sociology training and thought on Odum's ideas about race. Clearly, Johnson was the key influence on Odum's intellectual acceptance of liberal racial views, just as John Wesley Gordon was the primary influence on Odum's emotions about race. Johnson's musical gifts were also an important addition to Odum's work on African American folk song. In turn, however, Johnson's academic interests were profoundly influenced by Odum's interest in folklore and African American culture.

In fact, although music was an important part of Johnson's childhood, his early research in sociology at the University of Chicago focused entirely on race issues. His master's thesis topic was the Ku Klux Klan; on Wiley Sanders's recommendation he revised it and sent it to Odum. Odum published "A Sociological Interpretation of the New Ku Klux Klan Movement" in *The Journal of Social Forces* (May 1923) and also Johnson's paper on "The Northern Negro Migration and its Consequences" (March 1924). In 1924 Johnson and his wife were both teaching at Baylor College for Women in Texas when Odum invited Guy Johnson to be the first recipient of an assistantship at the IRSS. Johnson explains his reaction to the offer in his memoir *My Love Affair with Music and Other Personal Recollections* (1986): "I told him that Guion [his wife] and I were equally committed to careers, that she had a very happy job situation that she would be loath to give up unless she had an opportunity to pursue a doctorate. Odum's response was to offer Guion an assistantship too. We decided that this was an opportunity that we could not turn down" (25). Clearly, both Odum and Johnson had pretty enlightened gender-role views, as well as enlightened racial views, for their day.

Johnson's work with Odum on the folk-song books reawakened his interest in music. In his memoir he explains that while collecting from "black schools, strolling guitar players, and convict labor gangs" for the second book, "I was as much intrigued by the music as by the words of the songs and this time I got Odum to agree to my writing a chapter on 'Some Typical Negro Tunes.' Since I had had no training in composition or notation, I had to teach myself quickly how to get melodies on paper" (28).

In an interview Johnson recalled, "I always thought of myself as a sociologist and he did too." Johnson's impression of folklore was that it involved discussing variants and versions and he "always found this sort of thing a little tedious. This to me was not as interesting as the content, the themes, what was going on in the people's lives that developed these songs," and "it occurred to me once that I was really glad I had come into this from sociology instead of the standard folklorist approach . . . I got quite a few compliments from reviewers, say on the *John Henry* book, because they said it was something more than you usually got from a folklore study" (1985).

As a direct result of his research with Odum for the material in *Negro Workaday Songs,* Guy Johnson became interested in the John Henry legend and published his research on the ballad in *John Henry: Tracking Down a Negro Legend* (1929). Johnson's work in this book is especially interesting because it is the first full-length study of a single American folk song. Also, *John Henry* builds on the scientific foundation for folklore studies that Odum and Johnson established in *Negro Workaday Songs,* so the book is both an objective study of African American folk song, the product of field research, and an extremely readable and competent piece of folklore detective work.

Johnson opens *John Henry* with a statement of his mission "to bring together and co-ordinate as much actual folk material as possible and thus lay a foundation for various other approaches to the study of John Henry" (preface). He lists the known facts and legends about John Henry and concludes that (1) there probably was a steel driver named John Henry at Big Bend Tunnel; (2) he competed with a steam drill; and (3) he died soon after, probably from a fever (54).

Johnson disagrees with one popular theory—that John Henry is the same as John Hardy, a man hanged for murder in West Virginia in 1894—and he believes that the overlapping of the texts of ballads about each man comes from Hardy's story being patterned on John Henry, particularly because the song "John Henry" originated several years before "John Hardy" (62). Because the "tunes and rhythms" of the ballads are so different, Johnson thinks the Hardy ballad is of white Appalachian origin and concludes "the ballads as well as the men are separate entities" (67).

Johnson also speculates on the evolution of the John Henry song; he believes it was first a spontaneous hammer song with few details, then a printed ballad with expanded information. Johnson obtained what he believes is the only surviving early printed version of the ballad from a woman in north Georgia. This ballad text was written about 1900 by "Blankenship," and Johnson postulates that he was a white man who picked up the preexisting John Henry material and made a commercial ballad (85). Johnson includes numerous versions of the ballad, both texts and tunes.

Johnson closes his book with a discussion of the popularity and long-lasting appeal of the legend and ballad of John Henry. He notes that "the diffusion of the John Henry tradition among the Negro folk of all sections of the nation and, incidentally, among a large proportion of the white population, is a phenomenon of no mean importance." Even with his limited means of collecting data on John Henry, he had "come into the possession of something about him from practically every section of the United States" (146). Johnson speculates on one reason for the appeal of the song: "John Henry stands for something which the pick-and-shovel Negro idolizes—brute strength. He epitomizes the tragedy of man versus machine" (142). This quality in the legend also made Johnson's book appealing to many readers.

An important strength of Johnson's book is his explanation of the contexts in black culture for the dissemination of songs and stories about John Henry. In the last chapter of the book, titled "John Henry, the Hero," Johnson describes a storytelling session during a storm on the Sea Islands of South Carolina. One man complains that he cannot take his boat out in such weather, even though his family needs food, and his wife counters, "T'ink of ol' John Henry. . . . If he could die wid dat hammer in his hand, you ought not to fuss about rowin' two mile to git us somethin' to eat" (148). Her husband is inspired by the mention of John Henry and then tells all he knows about him. Johnson's guide is similarly inspired. Later, when they are rowing home through rough seas, Johnson asks if they will make it; his guide replies, "Yes-suh! I jus' been study about dat John Henry. If dat man could beat de steam, I t'ink I bring dis ol' boat back to dat landin' all right. If I don't, I'll die wid dese oar in my hand" (149). Johnson concludes that John Henry's tale continues "to capture the imagination of those who hear it for the first time" because "there is enough tragedy, enough humor, enough heroism in it to make it a story which will last" (150).

Johnson also notes that the John Henry legend is excellent material "for an epic poem, for a play, for an opera, for a Negro symphony. What more tragic theme than the theme of John Henry's martyrdom?" (150). Johnson's wish was answered, and after publication of his study, many "poems, play, musicals, ballets and sculptures were created around the John Henry theme" (*Research* 135). In fact, one of Johnson's informants told him there was a large stone sculpture of John Henry with hammer in hand outside the Big Bend Tunnel. It was fantasy at the time, but it is now actual fact, another tribute to the legend and to Johnson's research (*Research* 135).

Louise Pound's review of Johnson's book in the *Journal of American Folklore* was quite favorable. She believed that "the day of abstract, theoretical discussion of folk-song passes. . . . The future promises to see many investigations of selected traditional songs, current in special times and places among special folk-groups. It will be time for scholars to resume generalization when many such studies have been made" (126). Pound felt that Johnson's book might serve "as a model of research" because he "left no stone unturned in his efforts to determine the authenticity of his hero and to follow the history of the songs that glorify him" (126–27). The book is scientific, but "it is fascinating reading as well" (127).

Pound later helped mediate a controversy surrounding Johnson's John Henry book. Louis Chappell, who published his own study of John Henry in 1933, accused Johnson of plagiarizing some of his research. Chappell writes,

> In September, 1925, I investigated John Henry at Big Bend Tunnel, and in February, 1927, a 19-page report of my work there fell into the hands of Dr. Johnson. I had written the report to preserve my priority claims until I could complete a larger plan of investigation on the subject, and was trying to get it published at the University of North Carolina. The following is Dr. Johnson's only acknowledgement: "I wonder to what extent collectors have made John Henry famous at Big Bend! I know of at least two others who were trailing John Henry there before I made my visit." (6, n. 35)

D. K. Wilgus, in his book on folk-song scholarship, comments on Chappell's "carping" tone, but concludes that "his ugly charges remain unanswered" (398, n. 116).

In one of our interviews, Johnson commented on Chappell's accusation. Johnson did read Chappell's paper in the spring of 1927 and recommended that Odum publish the paper if Chappell would agree to cut about fifteen pages of "standard old-fashioned discussion of variants." Johnson fully expected Chappell to revise the paper and return it for publication, but neither he nor Odum heard from Chappell again and the paper was never published. Later that year Chappell wrote a "nasty letter to Odum," accusing Johnson of getting a list of interviewees for his book from Chappell's paper (interview 1986).

Johnson feels that Chappell was misled by the section in *Negro Workaday Songs* in which John Henry is described as a mythical character. Johnson says that he believed that John Henry was a real person, but "Odum thought it would make a good contrast to say Left Wing Gordon was a real character . . . [and] John Henry was just a mythical being" (interview 1986). By the time *Negro Workaday Songs* was published in 1926, Johnson was already collecting songs and had published advertisements in black newspapers for a printed copy of an old John

Henry ballad. He had also corresponded with potential informants at Big Bend Tunnel. Johnson went to West Virginia in June 1927 and collected material for his book.

Shortly after Chappell's book was published, he wrote a note to Louise Pound saying that Johnson had "prevaricated about interviewing a certain man" in West Virginia. Chappell maintained that Johnson could not have interviewed a Mr. Hendrick because he was quarantined during Johnson's visit. Johnson says that he had gone to Hendrick's house and asked his daughter if he could "stand in the door of the bedroom" and ask a few questions. He talked to Mr. Hendrick for a few minutes, but when it became obvious that his informant was tired, Johnson asked if he could send a letter with a list of questions for the daughter to ask her father; then she could write down the answers and return the letter to Johnson later. Johnson kept the dated letter he wrote to the daughter, which began "When I saw you yesterday . . ." and sent the letter to Louise Pound as proof that he had indeed interviewed Hendrick. She told Johnson that she thought the matter was ended, and it seems to be.

Johnson's work is one of the first successful folk-song studies because it is a full-length, well-documented, careful analysis of a single folk song. *John Henry* is based on research Odum and Johnson conducted together, but Johnson's individual folk-song work is much more thorough and scientific than these men's collaborative publications. *John Henry* has qualities not found in *The Negro and His Songs* and *Negro Workaday Songs,* including variants of song texts, tunes, and careful documentation of sources, as well as a discussion of the performance contexts of the song and accompanying tales. Johnson's work is also characterized by an appreciative but objective tone, illustrated in the closing paragraph of the book:

> Maybe there is no John Henry. One can easily doubt it. But there is a vivid, fascinating, tragic legend about him which Negro folk have kept alive and have cherished for more than half a century, and in so doing they have enriched the cultural life of America. (151)

## Johnson's St. Helena Island Research

Johnson was involved in another collaborative folklore project, a St. Helena Island study that produced three publications: *Black Yeomanry: Life on St. Helena Island* (Henry Holt, 1930), by T. J. Woofter Jr.; *A Social History of the Sea Islands* (UNC Press, 1930), by Guion Griffis Johnson; and *Folk Culture on St. Helena Island, S.C.* (UNC Press, 1930), by Guy Johnson. The St. Helena Island project was partly a political move by Odum to avoid controversy about the institute. Odum had recommended the appointment of Woofter as research assistant in April 1927, but, unfortunately, during that summer he was arrested in Virginia for drunken driving, and some faculty members felt he should not be allowed to work at the university. Odum and two friends of Woofter decided that a research project on the Sea Islands could legitimately occupy him off-campus for a time (*Research* 50–51).

The project was also an important "cultural isolate" study because the St. Helena Island blacks, who spoke the distinctive Gullah dialect, "had been isolated from the mainstream of American culture for sixty years." Folklorists feared that the planned bridge across Port Royal Sound would quickly assimilate the islanders and their folk culture into modern American life, so social science research in the area seemed immediately important (*Research* 52). The books by Woofter and Guion G. Johnson are sociological and historical studies, respectively, but Guy Johnson concentrated on the speech, music, and tales of the islanders.

In *Folk Culture on St. Helena Island,* Johnson explains his conclusions about the origins of the Gullah dialect. He writes, "Gullah has been called the most African of any of our Negro dialects, yet it can be traced back in practically every detail to English dialect speech" (6). Johnson theorizes that African slaves learned their English from American settlers with origins in the English peasant class (7). He supports his theory with a detailed phonological and grammatical analysis of the dialect, attempting to show that most of its distinctive characteristics can be traced to the dialects of southern England, although he does note a few words of clear African origin: "okra," "gumbo," and "yam," for example (57).

Many of Johnson's assertions were later refuted in Lorenzo Turner's fifteen-year study of the Gullah dialect, published in *Africanisms in the Gullah Dialect* (1949). Turner analyzed the phonetic, syntactic, and morphological features of Gullah to prove that it "is a creolized form of English revealing survivals from many of the African languages spoken by the slaves" (v). He accounts for the fact that Johnson and "others who contend that Gullah is derived solely from English reveal in their writings no knowledge whatsoever of the many thousand African personal names still used by the Gullahs," noting that "when talking to strangers the Gullah Negro is likely to use speech that is essentially English in vocabulary" (12).

More recent scholarship also emphasizes the Africanisms in the Gullah dialect. Charles Joyner, in *Down by the Riverside: A South Carolina Slave Community* (1984), comments that "whatever else might be said of the relationships between black and white speech in America, Gullah—as spoken by the last generation of slaves—followed a different set of grammatical rules than did English. . . . However much Gullah and English may have shared the same vocabulary, Gullah and English were not the same language" (202).

Johnson's discussion of the African American spiritual in *Folk Culture* also aroused controversy. The origins of the spiritual had been discussed at length by many music scholars before Johnson's work, but he had the advantage of studying an isolated folk group whose most popular form of religious music was the spiritual. Johnson cites historical, textual, and musical evidence that the spirituals were largely derived from white religious folk songs, particularly those sung at mid-nineteenth-century camp meetings that were attended by both whites and blacks. He cites words common to both black and white religious folk song and the use of the gapped or pentatonic scale in both as evidence that "spirituals are not different musically from white folk tunes" (127).

Johnson comments briefly on some of the rhythmical differences between black and white religious song and the significance of two-part time in black spirituals: "It is so intimately connected with their habit of swaying the body, patting the feet, and clapping the hands while singing. . . . This habit may well represent the survival of African tempo patterns" (114). Johnson states that rhythm is the major contribution of blacks to the spiritual genre, along with "the preservation of a large body of folk song which might otherwise have been extinct by now" (129).

Johnson fails to discuss the ring shout, a specific rhythmical performance style found among the Sea Islanders and described later by other folklorists, but he does mention the "leader-chorus pattern" of singing, although he ascribes it to the way new songs were taught to the illiterate islanders rather than to what we now know is a particularly African musical performance style (94).

George Pullen Jackson, in *White and Negro Spirituals* (1943), confirms Johnson's ideas. According to D. K. Wilgus, Jackson's book "firmly established the contention that the melodic core of Negro religious songs developed from white spirituals" (356). Most folk-song scholars now believe that blacks and whites were introduced to both styles of religious singing during the camp meetings of the nineteenth-century surge of Protestant revivalism. However, a number of readers objected to Johnson's ideas about the white origins of African American spirituals, among them blacks who claimed he was trying to rob them of their heritage, and scholar Melville Herskovits, who felt Johnson was ignoring the survival of Africanisms that must be more prominent on St. Helena Island and the other Sea Islands than anywhere in the United States. Johnson explained that although Herskovits had done some limited fieldwork in Africa, he "had no sense of the continuity of the white folk culture"; therefore he assumed anything strange must be African in origin (interview 1985). Johnson says he did try to emphasize African elements in spirituals, particularly the "manner of singing, rhythm, and probably a lot of the tunes"—all traits that would be more likely to survive an intercontinental emigration than words. He said he finally concluded that

> What you have now is really a new culture that the blacks have, you
> have (a) the white culture, (b) the African, and the interaction, that's the
> thing, you've got a new product now which is neither, it's something new
> you see and that's basically what I thought the spirituals were: they're
> not strictly white music or African music; they're Afro-American. (inter-
> view 1985)

Contemporary folk-song scholars have come to agree with Johnson
and the current emphasis today is on the amount of acculturation between the two races as well as on separate European and African cultural survivals.

In assessing Johnson's folklore work, it is important to note that he
did not come to the University of North Carolina with the intention of
becoming a folklorist. In fact, he felt that his own studies in race relations were being sidetracked by Odum's folk-song projects (interview
1985). Johnson also felt that *The Negro and His Songs* and *Negro Workaday
Songs* were not sound scientific documents, so he tried to make certain that his own folk-song studies were more carefully documented.
However, just as Johnson criticizes Herskovits for his limited knowledge of white folk culture, so Johnson's work is sometimes flawed by
his limited knowledge of African culture, especially in his discussion
of Gullah dialect. Nevertheless, because of his "modern" sociological
training and his gift for music, Johnson made important contributions
to the field of folklore studies. In many ways his work surpassed the
folk-song research of his mentor, Howard Odum, because he was able
to be more objective about the material.

## Paul Green's Folk Plays

Paul Green, like Howard Odum, came from a rural folk background
that certainly influenced the subject matter of his early plays. It also
seems apparent, however, when we look at the careers of these two
men, that their friendship influenced the work of both. Paul Green's
career, for instance, is a clear embodiment of Odum's literary and social ideals.

One of the liberal spirits who attracted Odum to Chapel Hill in the first place was Edwin Greenlaw, chairman of the English department. In 1918, two years before Odum came to UNC, Greenlaw invited Frederick Koch, founder of the North Dakota folk-play movement, to continue his work at the University of North Carolina. Koch founded the Carolina Playmakers in 1918, and it soon became a thriving group of writers and actors (Adams 18).

In the first publication of the Playmakers, *Carolina Folk-Plays: First Series,* founder Koch describes the group's aim: "To serve as an experimental theatre for the young playwright seeking to translate into fresh dramatic forms the traditions and present-day life of the people" (vi). Koch writes that the plays in this volume are "wholly native–simple plays of the locality, of common experience and of common interest," and that "the stories and characters are drawn by the writers from their own tradition, and from their observation of the lives of their own people" (xi). Koch believed that a "strong folk-consciousness" persisted in North Carolina, which "should be cherished in a new republic of active literature" (xxix).

Koch developed his ideas about folk drama in North Dakota, but at the University of North Carolina they came to fruition, at least partly because he found a climate conducive to the flourishing of such democratic artistic ideals. Many of Koch's colleagues at the university were equally interested in folk studies and supported his work, among them, Howard Odum. Walter Spearman, in his history *The Carolina Playmakers: The First Fifty Years* (1970), comments that Koch came to know many faculty members "who could tell him stories and traditions of North Carolina and who became strong supporters of The Carolina Playmakers: Archibald Henderson, Howard W. Odum, . . . [and] Arthur Palmer Hudson" (11).

In an article in *Southern Folklore Quarterly* entitled "Folklore and the Drama: The Carolina Playmakers and Their 'Folk Plays,' " Charles G. Zug comments on Koch's use of the term "folk" to describe plays written by the Playmakers. Zug finds that Koch does not use the term "folk play" in the traditional sense, to describe mummers' or miracle plays;

rather, he uses the term to emphasize "the proper content for his folk plays: folktale, folksong, superstition, custom, and folk dialect" (286). Zug concludes that the playwrights used these materials functionally, "to develop or enrich the plot, setting, atmosphere, characters, and themes" (291).

Most of the early plays written and produced by the Carolina Playmakers at UNC and published in *Carolina Folk-Plays: First Series* (1922) use folklore functionally to "advance the plot, to characterize, to provide structure" rather than to raise questions about society (Cohen 243). For example, *When Witches Ride: A Play of Folk Superstition,* by Elizabeth Lay, describes three men playing cards at a crossroads store during "witch weather." When Phoebe, an old woman purported to be a witch, arrives, two of the men are terrified. Only the third man, Jake, refuses to believe in witchcraft—until Phoebe dies and leaves him her toad, a sign that he is witched. The play is entertaining but does nothing more than dramatize superstition.

The play *"Dod Gast Ye Both!": A Comedy of Mountain Moonshiners,* by Hubert C. Heffner, describes the antics of a family of mountain moonshiners and promulgates the popular idea of the folk as simple, comic people. The mountaineer's daughter tricks her father into allowing her to marry a man he thought was a "revenoor." His frustrated but good-humored blessing gives the play its name.

*Off Nags Head or The Bell Buoy: A Tragedy of the North Carolina Coast,* by Dougald McMillan, presents the surprise conclusion to a mysterious legend that the daughter of Aaron Burr survived a shipwreck off the North Carolina coast but suffered amnesia for the rest of her life. The folk elements of the story, the dialect and setting, are merely quaint details rather than the basis for deeper religious, psychological, or social truths.

Only two plays in the first volume by the Carolina Playmakers contain some vestige of social comment and use folklore functionally to "raise questions about the nature of society" (Cohen 243). Harold Williamson's play *Peggy: A Tragedy of the Tenant Farmer* describes the harsh treatment of Peggy and her mother by their landlord after the father dies. Peggy has been wooed and deceived by the landlord's son; in the end she must marry a man she does not love in order to save her family.

One other play in this volume contains a hint of the social concerns that were to dominate the plays of Paul Green, ultimately the most famous playwright of the group. His play *The Last of the Lowries: A Play of the Croatan Outlaws of Robeson County, North Carolina* describes the end of the Croatan Indian tribe, whose deaths are partially ascribed to prejudice. One character comments, "That's the way with them white folks. They do all they kin agin' us poor Croatans, 'cause we's jes' injuns, they says—though we knows better" (120). This comment also contains a hint of the theory that the Croatans are what remain of Sir Walter Raleigh's Lost Colony, a theory that forms the basis for Green's symphonic drama, *The Lost Colony* (1937). Both Williamson's and Green's plays comment on social injustice toward the poor and toward nonwhite racial groups; Green was to expand on these themes in many of his subsequent folk plays.

Green, in fact, was the one Playmaker who consistently used folklore in his plays as the basis for social comment. Green's interest in the folk can be traced to various influences on his life. He was born on March 17, 1894, to a North Carolina farming family. Green enrolled at the University of North Carolina in September 1916; after fighting in World War I, he returned to Chapel Hill in 1919 to resume his studies and came under the tutelage of Frederick Koch. Agatha Adams, in her biography *Paul Green of Chapel Hill* (1951), speculates that "had not the Playmakers been at that time the most lively creative group on the campus, Green might not have become a playwright at all" (19). Green eventually married fellow Playmaker Elizabeth Lay, and they moved to Cornell, where he continued his studies in philosophy. The Greens returned to Chapel Hill when Paul was offered a faculty position in the Philosophy Department, and there he also continued his work as a playwright.

Green was actually a folklorist as well as an artist. In his "Tentative Memorandum: Regional and Folk Portraiture as Materials for Social

Science," Odum lists Paul and Elizabeth Lay Green's book *Folk Beliefs of the Carolina Sandhills* as among those important folklore studies (2). Green also prepared another folklore collection titled *Words and Ways: Stories and Incidents from My Cape Fear Valley Folklore Collection* (North Carolina Folklore Society 1968). He writes in the foreword that the material in the book comes from years of "collecting the folklore of my people—noting down their speech, beliefs, customs, anecdotes, ballads, epitaphs, legends, proverbs, stories, superstitions, herb cures, games and the like, as well as gathering biographies of many a gnarled and crusted character, real and imaginary" (iii). Green also contributed several entries on weather beliefs to the *Frank C. Brown Collection of North Carolina Folklore* and used these entries in his plays.

In his collection of essays titled *The Hawthorn Tree* (1943), Green writes about his interest in the folk. He states, "Most of the plays I have written can be designated as folk plays, and I know this seems a narrow boundary. Perhaps it is, but since the 'folk' are the people who seem to matter most to me, I have little interest in trying to deal with others who are more foreign and therefore less real to me" (31). He adds a comment worthy of the English Romantic poets: "Those who live as it were with their feet in the earth and their head bare to the storms . . . these develop a wisdom of living which seems to me more real and beautiful than those who develop their values and ambitions from rubbing shoulders in a crowded city" (33). However, in the essay "Folk Drama Defined," Green does distinguish between the art of the folk and his writings about the folk. Folk drama is not folk art: "Both the dramatist and the actors who create the folk-play may in no sense be of 'the folk,' and their piece may never be seen or heard of by the type of people it portrays, and yet it is folk-drama if its material is such" (98).

A folklorist defines a folk play as an artistic product *of* the folk, not merely an artistic description *about* the folk. However, Green's plays do fulfill Howard Odum's criteria for literary regional portraiture that helps to discover and explain cultural differences in America. In fact, although Green's early interest in the folk and his early artistic efforts were largely influenced by his background and his tutelage by Koch, a careful examination of Green's folk plays shows interesting parallels between his work and Odum's research and fiction, not only because they use much of the same folklore in their work but also because Green uses folklore to comment on many of the social problems that concerned Odum.

Most of Green's biographers and critics have not credited Howard Odum with influencing Green's interests in folklore or social criticism. Adams points to Green's use of folk material for social comment in his early plays. She describes themes in these plays that he later developed fully: "the bitter fate of the Negro, the Negro's ambition to rise, his frustrations, the white man's injustice and blind cruelty, love between Negro and white, the angry resentments bred by the pressures of small neighborhoods, the defeated aspirations of the tenant farmer, the tragedies caused by intense yet ignorant religious feeling, the decay of old families in the Old South" (31). In his book *Paul Green* (1971), Vincent Kenny notes that sociological studies by Howard W. Odum "forced upon America a new look at the Negro. Such sociological studies on race did not disclose new information for Green; they merely supplied a scientific basis for what had been implicit in his writings from the early 1920s" (66).

However, something of a mentor relationship did exist between Odum and Green. That there was a social and intellectual relationship between the two men is clear from several letters about family get-togethers, and the correspondence also indicates Green's respect for the older scholar. Green generally addresses Odum as "Dr. Odum" (letter from Green to Odum, January 21, 1925) or "Professor Odum" (letter from Green to Odum, September 11, 1933), while Odum's letters to Green often read "Dear Green" (letters from Odum to Green, July 1, 1925; August 6, 1930).

Guy Johnson saw similarities in Odum's and Green's personalities; they were both "active, dynamic, had lots of new ideas," but Green was "more authentically folk." Johnson believes that Green's plays were "authentic folk-portrayals." Green was also "very interested" in the work that Odum and Johnson were doing in the 1920s and '30s (interview 1985). In fact, Odum asked Green to read the manuscript of *Rainbow Round My Shoulder*. Green's response in a letter dated January 14, 1928, contains an interesting artistic analysis of the work:

> I have read the manuscript . . . with great interest and delight. So far as I can see you have done a fine and lasting job. This roustabout, who for so many years has wandered around in our land as well as in our consciousness, has at last been set forth in the light and in the rounded form of art, and will, I have little doubt, become a character synonomous [*sic*] with a type. You have firmly set this lonely, disconsolate, joyous, broiling, whooping, working, singing Black Ulysses in the gallery of figures where Uncle Remus, Paul Bunyan, Babbitt and others abide. I believe that, and I believe that he will not die from us now for many a long season. Here's to you. (Odum Papers)

Although Odum did not serve as a formal mentor to Green in the same way he did to Guy Johnson, Green certainly profited from his friendship with the older professor, and many of Green's early plays parallel both Odum's social concerns and his interest in folklore. In fact, the time frame of Green's interest in folklore is almost exactly the same as Odum's. After 1935, Odum concentrated on developing his theory of new regionalism, and Green began writing his symphonic dramas, but from 1920 until 1935, both men were involved in research and writing about folklore, particularly the black folk culture of the South and of North Carolina.

Green and Odum also knew much of the same folklore, especially folk songs, and employed it in their literary work. Green's folk plays contain black folk music, and some of these same songs are found in Odum and Johnson's folk-song collections. One version of a song that Odum and Johnson cite is found in Green's play *Your Fiery Furnace*, an earlier version of *In Abraham's Bosom* published in the volume *Lonesome Road* (1926). In the play, Doug, Abraham's son, sings a song for his grandmother:

Look down, look down dat lonesome road,
De hacks all dead in line.
Some give nickel, some give dime
To bury dis po' body o' mine. (197)

The same song, with the tune, is found in the final three-act version of *In Abraham's Bosom* (306). The version of this song that Odum and Johnson cite in *The Negro and His Songs* is almost exactly the same:

Look down po' lonesome road,
Hacks all dead in line.
Some give nickel, some give dime,
To bury dis po' body o' mine. (194)

These words are the last verse of a song that begins "I love that man, O God, I do" (194), and Odum and Johnson include it in a chapter on social songs.

In *Your Fiery Furnace*, Doug plays the song as entertainment for his grandmother; she says "Ain't dat de old-time stuff?" (196), but his mother says she is in no mood for such songs and asks him to play "my old piece," a song about Judgment Day (205). Those who were unfamiliar with the complete text of the "Lonesome Road" song might conclude it is a religious burial song; Green knew the song and put it in the correct context in his plays.

Although Green may well have used some of the songs he found in Odum and Johnson's books in his plays, other songs came from different sources, for he and they encountered different variants of the same songs. Both Green and Odum and Johnson cite somewhat different versions of a song about a rounder named Brady. Again, in *In Abraham's Bosom*, Douglass sings the song to entertain his grandmother, Muh Mack (94). Green also includes the tune to this song at the end of the book (307). The version of "Brady" that Odum and Johnson cite in *The Negro and His Songs* has an additional verse (209).

Green was also familiar with the black folk song that Odum used for the title of his novel *Rainbow Round My Shoulder.* In *Roll, Sweet Chariot* (1935), Farrow, one of the boarders at Old Quiviene's house, sings:

> Everywhere I look, I look this mawning,
> Looks like rain, Lord, look-a like rain.
> I got rainbow round my shoulder. (5)

Green again includes the tune of this song at the end of the book (97). Odum and Johnson's version has another verse that ends the song with the refrain, "Ain't gonna rain" (*Negro Workaday Songs* 2). Two different tunes for this song, which are also different from the tune Green notes, are found in chapter 14 of their book (249).

Green, like Johnson, also distinguishes between the two different ballads, "John Hardy" and "John Henry." In *The Last of the Lowries,* published in *The Lord's Will and Other Carolina Plays* (1925), Henry Berry sings three verses of the song that Johnson felt was certainly a white ballad. Green's version of "John Hardy" also has no similarities to the "John Henry" ballad in wording or in theme.

Clearly, Green and Odum were both interested in folk music, and Green may have used some songs in his plays that he obtained from Odum and Johnson's collections. The most important connection between Green and Odum's work, however, is their interest in similar social topics. This shows up in both the research and fiction of Odum and in the plays of Green, and in their similar use of folklore in literature to comment on social problems. For example, many topics in Green's plays are linked to social science studies at the University of North Carolina during the 1920s and '30s. In his thesis, "Social Problems in the Plays of Paul Green" (1964), Daniel Linney describes three social topics found in Green's plays: religion, education, and class and race relations. Almost all of Green's early plays, in fact, deal with social problems that were being investigated by Odum or other IRSS faculty. Two of these topics, religion and race relations, were important concerns of Odum as well.

Several of Green's plays depict fundamentalist religion, a topic that concerned Odum and an issue that caused problems for him. In January 1924 the *Journal of Social Forces* published two articles that offended members of the Presbyterian Ministerial Association. They called the pieces "a serious offense against the faith, feelings and life work of the Christian people of North Carolina." A year later, another ministerial committee criticized two other articles published in *Social Forces*. They objected to Luther L. Bernard's view that "gods were mythological human creations" and to Harry Elmer Barnes's denial of "the divine origins of revelation and of conscience" and his call for "the replacement of moral beliefs by a scientific system in which the clergy would have no part" (Johnson, *Research* 41).

Odum stood up for the principle of academic freedom during the ensuing controversy, although he wrote a letter of apology to the governor of North Carolina, accepting full responsibility for the articles as editor of the journal. As a result of his tangle with religious leaders, he "gave up his dream of making the *Journal* an instrument for enlarging the horizons of the average citizen," according to Johnson (*Research* 42).

Green also wanted to educate his audiences to the dangers of religious fundamentalism, and in several of his folk plays he dramatizes the religious forces with which Odum came in conflict. In *The Lord's Will* (1922), Lem Adams, a country preacher and tenant farmer, is a man consumed by religious fervor.[1] Adams neglects his wife, Mary, and their child. The child becomes ill while playing outside in the cold because Lem "didn't have no time to fool with her"; he was too busy "reading the Bible and working at his sermons" (13). His wife is afraid to get the doctor even when a neighbor says the child has "got pneumonia in both sides" (23), because "Lem don't believe in medicine; . . . [he] says you must have faith" (24). Mary ultimately defies Lem, saying, "I love to work on the farm and live respectable and have things a woman likes. . . . And you're fit for nothing but preaching and praying and reading that old Bible" (42). But she is too late: the child dies. Green's portrait of a man who neglects life on earth in pursuit of the life hereafter is unremittingly grim.

A similar character gets more humorous treatment in *Quare Medicine* (1928).[2] Mattie Jernigan, an extremely pious woman, makes life miserable for her husband, Henry, and his father. They are afraid to put their feet on the clean hearth, chew tobacco, or comment on Mattie's sending Henry's coat to "them there Hindoos" (53). Old Man Jernigan tells his son, "This religious mess is gonna kill Mattie off ef you don't git up manhood enough to stop it" (53). When Doctor Immanuel, a patent-medicine vendor, stops by, the old man takes matters into his own hands and asks the doctor for a "manhood potion" for Henry. Henry drinks the potion, realizes it is only water, and forces Mattie to drink a potion to make her meek. He finally makes it clear to Mattie that both draughts were harmless, but they have done their job; Henry says, "I'm cured, I'm boss," and Mattie meekly accepts her new role (78). Religious piety has been foiled.

*The Field God* (1927) is one of Green's most powerful plays. The protagonist, Hardy Gilchrist, a successful farmer, marries his pretty niece, Rhoda, after the death of his sickly wife. Soon his luck takes a turn for the worse, and his pious neighbors try to convince him he is being punished for the sin of pride. Gilchrist almost breaks as the preacher prays, "Stretch him on the rack, for it is the way to his salvation. Already thou has laid a hand on his little son—keep it on him—take him away to make his proud heart yield" (269). But Rhoda interferes with the redemptive process, telling the preacher, "He's a thousand times better than you all, better than anybody, better than God is" (275). When their child dies, both Gilchrist and Rhoda blame God, the "God of hate" (296), who "comes when I'm gone and takes away my child" (297). The reaffirmation at the end of the play is not one of faith in God but of human love. Gilchrist declares, "Their way is the way of death. Ours is the way of love and that is life" (298). Finally, he says, "We are God—Man is God," and Rhoda replies "You are my God" (301). In this play Green dramatizes some of the attitudes found in *Social Forces,* including the idea that human, not godly, love is the greatest good.

One of Green's early plays deals with miscegenation, a sensitive racial issue that Odum never openly broached in his work. *White Dresses*

(1926) had to be cancelled from the Playmakers' bill in 1921 because of the controversy it aroused.[3] The play describes the plight of a young black woman, Mary McLean, who is in love with her white landlord's son. The landlord, Henry Morgan, threatens to throw Mary and her grandmother out of their house unless Mary consents to marry Jim Matthews, another black tenant. At the end of the play, the grandmother reveals why Mary must do as she is told; Henry Morgan is her father and his son is her half-brother. The grandmother's words at the end of the play sum up Mary's untenable position and the position of all blacks in a white-dominated society: "I know yo' feelings, chile, but you's gut to smother 'em in, you's gut to smother 'em in" (68).

*The End of the Row* (1926) and its sequel, *The Goodbye* (1928), also deal with the topic of miscegenation.[4] The heroine of these plays, Lalie, has two problems—dealing with the white race and dealing with fellow blacks. She is an intelligent person and has ambitions to educate herself and other blacks, but she meets with opposition from both races. Lalie's life is further complicated by her love affair with her white landlord, Ed Roberts. In *The Goodbye*, we learn that Lalie and Ed have a child, but he has decided to be "respectable" and marry a white woman who can bear white heirs. Ed wants Lalie to remain his mistress, but she refuses. He tells her she has been "everything" to him, but she replies, "not enough" (305). He asks, "Ain't it natural for a man to want—to want a family, children?" (305). Both plays are a moving commentary on the plight of blacks, who are unable to choose their place in the world, and the problems for interracial couples during this time, who must either suffer censure or separate.

One of Green's well-known characters is Abraham McCranie in the Pulitzer Prize–winning play, *In Abraham's Bosom* (1927).[5] The play tells the story of McCranie, a tenant farmer who, like Lalie, has aspirations of becoming a teacher and improving the lives of his fellow blacks. He endures misery, hardship, and ridicule; he is opposed by blacks who think he is "uppity" and by whites who think he is dangerous. His own son rebels against him and becomes a petty criminal, and his wife, though loyal to the end, is near death from hard work and suffering.

The play ends when Abraham, enraged by whites who do not allow him to hold a meeting about a school for blacks, kills his white half-brother. A posse comes to his home, and he is shot to death as he walks out on the porch to meet them. As Abraham dies, he speaks the words that are the theme of the play: "We got to be free, freedom of the soul and of the mind. Ignorance means sin and sin means destruction. Freedom!" (139).

Linney comments that all of Green's major Southern black characters are mulatto (62). His point raises some interesting questions about Green's own racial views. Does Green see miscegenation as the most serious racial problem in the South, or are his important black characters of mixed race because he believes only people who are at least half-white are capable of aspiring to a better way of life? The problems that the mixed-race characters Lalie and Abraham McCranie have with other blacks who have no desire to change their lives supports the latter idea. Green may have been more liberal than Odum in his willingness to portray interracial relationships, but it is not clear from the evidence of his plays that he believed in the complete equality of the races any more than Odum.

Another social problem under investigation by members of the IRSS was the prison "chain gang." Jesse F. Steiner and Roy M. Brown published *The North Carolina Chain Gang: A Study of County Convict Work* (1927), where they pointed to "the degrading spectacle of men working in public in chains" as not the least of the problems with such a system (Johnson, *Research* 242). Green waged a lifelong personal campaign against the death penalty and the North Carolina prison system, and in several plays he describes the horrors of the chain gang. One such play, *Roll, Sweet Chariot: A Symphonic Play of the Negro People* (1935), is probably the last of the plays Green wrote that can be termed "folk play."

The setting of *Roll, Sweet Chariot* is Old Quiviene Lockley's boarding house in the black settlement of Potter's Field, which is soon to be razed to build a new road. The main plot centers on Tom Sterling, who has become the lover of Milly Wilson while her husband, Bantam, is serving time on the chain gang. John Henry arrives at the boarding house with mysteriously gained knowledge of everyone who lives there. It turns out that he is the accomplice of Bantam, who has been recently released from jail. Bantam returns to claim his right to spend the night with Milly, and Sterling, enraged by jealousy and Bantam's harsh treatment of Milly, kills Bantam. At the end of the play, both Sterling and John Henry are serving on the chain gang; Sterling kills one of the guards and is shot to death.

Green's functional use of folklore to raise questions about society is at its best in *Roll, Sweet Chariot.* He clearly bases the semi-mythical hero of the play, John Henry, on the black hero of the same name, implying an important quality that both Odum and Green admired in the folk, the ability to endure and rise above the profound injustices of the society in which they live. Howard Pearce notes that Green "had evidently gained some recognition for his interest in the John Henry legend, for Guy B. Johnson in the preface to his *John Henry: Tracking Down a Negro Legend* . . . acknowledged Green's having read the manuscript of his book" (71, n. 25). In this instance, at least, Green may have influenced Johnson's work rather than vice versa.

In an earlier version of the play, titled *In the Valley* (1928), John Henry's mythical and heroic qualities are illustrated in an exchange he has with Farrow early in the play. He introduces himself to the other boarders at Old Quiviene's boarding house, and Farrow asks, "Any kin to the John Henry was such a steel-driving fool?" Henry answers, "Mebbe the same man, but no fool" (9). Farrow declares triumphantly, "Cain't be. He done daid" and sings:

Dis heah de hammer killed John Henry,
Killed him daid, boys, killed him daid.
Busted de brains all outen my pardner,
In de haid, boys, in de haid. (9)

In the comparable scene in *Roll, Sweet Chariot,* John Henry sings after Farrow:

Heard mighty rumbling, heard mighty rumbling,
Heard mighty rumbling under the ground.

Must be John Henry turning round.
Nine pound hammer, nine pound hammer,
Can't kill me, well, it can't kill me.
Nine pound hammer couldn't kill me. (26)

John Henry also illustrates the enduring quality of the folk; after Sterling kills the guard and is killed himself, it is John Henry who leads the people of Potter's Field in their hopeful hymn and work song:

They call their Jesus–hanh–
They say their Jesus–hanh–
They mean King Jesus–hanh–
Eigh, Lord! (92–93)

In an article in the *Southern Literary Journal,* Howard Pearce writes that in *Roll, Sweet Chariot,* as in *In Abraham's Bosom* and *The Field God,* an important theme is "the problem of justice, but in none of them is justice precisely worked out in the end" (76). The conclusion of *Roll, Sweet Chariot* "affirms, not justice, but hope" (77). Green, like Odum, is hopeful for the chances of social reform; he is also hopeful that his plays may aid in that reform. However, Green's willingness to discuss the problems does not mean he came any closer than Odum to finding solutions.

In many ways Green fulfilled Odum's literary ideals. Odum recognized the literary weakness of his own fiction, but he felt that one of the best ways of "proving this puzzle" of American culture was through the study and writing of folk and regional literature (*Folk, Region, and Society* 194). Green espoused many of the same ideals as Odum, and he also used folklore to portray many of the problems under investigation by Odum and other members of the IRSS. Whether Green was directly influenced by Odum or not, the two men certainly shared a desire to link folklore and social concerns in their respective fields, and it seems likely that they both profited from having a friend and colleague with similar goals and views.

## Odum as Academic Mentor

A number of historians have discussed Odum's contributions to the milieu of the University of North Carolina during the first half of the twentieth century. In addition to his influence over publications by the UNC Press, he was an important academic mentor to a number of young scholars, not only Guy Johnson and Paul Green but also Johnson's wife, Guion, for whom Odum provided assistantship money for graduate work, and T. J. Woofter, whose career was saved by Odum's intervention, as described earlier in this chapter. Others who benefited from Odum's direct support include Rupert Vance, Arthur Raper, Harriet Herring, Jennings Rhyne, Roy M. Brown, and Wiley B. Sanders. Daniel Singal concludes that when these younger scholars and disciples of Odum "began moving beyond mere description to analyze specific Southern problems like lynching, mill villages, and sharecropping with an eye to drawing causal connections and assigning responsibility, Odum could encourage but not join them" (116). Still, Singal acknowledges Odum's importance as a transitional figure at the beginning of the modernist period.

What emerges from a study of Odum's folklore work, however, is a portrait of a much more liberal person in private than in public. Singal quotes from Arthur Raper's memories of Odum in the classroom:

> Odum . . . he was just so full of questions—we had a course with him when he frankly the whole way through . . . hardly made a single statement. Asked questions. Now, when the textile industry comes to the South, what kind of wages will they pay in connection with what they were paying up there? What will they do with the Negro? Will he work at all or if he does work, what jobs will he work at? How about labor unions? Will they permit labor unions here? If they won't permit labor unions here, why won't they permit labor unions here? . . . Question, question, question, the whole way through. (129)

Odum's Socratic approach to teaching clearly touched on subjects that are still a matter of debate in the South; his teaching methods also inspired his students to try to find answers to these difficult questions.

Arthur Raper, for example, eventually published "the only close study of lynching that has been done in the last two generations," according to historian Joel Williamson (490).

While Singal and others have noted Odum's public retreat from controversial subjects during his middle age, his collaborative folklore work with Johnson and John Wesley Gordon provide evidence that privately his racial and political views were quite radical for the time. Singal concludes that Odum was "an artist, not an activist; a teacher, not a planner" (152). Not only is Odum's private journey toward racial tolerance a lesson in itself; as a teacher and artist his influence on the racial views, scholarship, and political activism of many others was extraordinary.

# CHAPTER SIX

# Mentoring and Collaboration as Keys to Cultural Understanding

n assessing Odum's contributions to the study of African American folklore and culture, two general topics emerge: mentoring and collaboration.

## Mentoring: Odum's Intellectual Legacy

Howard Washington Odum was among the most important and original of the Southern intellectuals who began to take a new look at the South after World War I. He helped usher in a new era in the region, both as a policymaker at the University of North Carolina and as an author of revolutionary works. As chairman of the University of North Carolina's first sociology department, director of the Institute for Research in Social Science, and member of the board of directors of the University of North Carolina Press, he influenced university policy and direction. He also made significant contributions to the field of sociology in general, particularly as founder of the journal *Social Forces* (1922) and as the author of *Southern Regions of the United States* (1936). Finally, he made important contributions to the field of folklore, in part because of his interdisciplinary approach to folk material and his desire to use his studies to improve social conditions in the South.

Both contemporary and modern assessments of Odum's achievements are favorable. Wayne D. Brazil, an Odum biographer, has written that Odum's "activities and publications between 1920 and 1930 probably contributed more than any other person's to earning Chapel Hill's reputation as a progressive university and the regional center of scholarly productivity" (iv).

George B. Tindall, a renowned University of North Carolina historian, discusses Odum's most important contributions to the South in a 1958 article in the *Journal of Social History*: (1) Odum's organizational and administrative contributions to the university; (2) his body of descriptive writings "presenting a picture of Southern folk, black and white, that is unmatched anywhere else for its perceptiveness, in a range all the way from prose-poetry depiction to general statistical analysis and set in a context of historical development"; (3) his papers that can be used for studies of the South's development; and (4) his theory of regionalism (303–5).

In his book *The Ethnic Southerners* (1976), Tindall analyzes the importance of Odum's regionalism theory:

> Regionalism is a means of synthesis of all the social sciences and, to
> some extent, of the humanities. It is the method whereby one can study
> society and see it whole, not in bits and snatches from the viewpoint of
> some narrow specialty. Yet, it is more than that. It is a program of action.
> It is an approach whereby the regions may be integrated into the
> national whole without losing their differentiation. (103)

Tindall's assessment of Odum's contributions to sociology and Southern history apply to his endeavors in the field of folklore as well. Odum's background as a classicist and his training in sociology and psychology enabled him to approach folk studies from an interdisciplinary standpoint. This approach allowed him to transcend the work of most previous collectors of Southern folklore, who, as humanists, were interested mainly in the texts of folk songs as poetry rather than as sociological and psychological reflections of a culture. This is not to say that Odum did not appreciate the art of the folklore he collected; rather, he was interested in folklore as both an artistic and social product of a culture. In fact, Odum's method of combining the fields of the humanities and the social sciences in his study of folklore anticipated the methodological trends of folklorists later in the century.

Odum's family background and education probably contributed a great deal to his ability to approach folk studies both humanistically and scientifically. Both his boyhood experiences in northern Georgia and the Christian ethic of brotherhood that he learned from his parents, as well as his studies with Thomas Pierce Bailey and G. Stanley Hall, helped him formulate his belief that research in Southern folklore and literature could play an important role in social reform. Of course, Odum's early folk-song collections had a political purpose as well; he wanted the first publication from the Institute for Research in Social Science to be as generally interesting and noncontroversial as possible, and he believed a study of black folk songs would serve that purpose. His collaboration on two African American folk-song collections with his student and colleague Guy Johnson benefited both men professionally and personally.

Ultimately, Odum and Johnson's two collections of black folk song are important achievements in the field of folklore because of the number of songs they collected, their attempts to represent the variety of black folk song, their appreciation of the artistry and creativity of black folk musicians, and their analysis of the social and psychological functions of folk song in Southern black culture. Also, the folk-song studies of Odum and Johnson were pioneering works because they were the first academics to focus on black secular songs, particularly work songs, and Odum was one of the first collectors of blues.

In addition to their importance to the field of folklore, Odum and Johnson's two folk-song collections are significant because they provide a portrait of the development of a Southern intellectual's views of race during the first half of the twentieth century. A careful examination of *The Negro and His Songs* and *Negro Workaday Songs* proves that Odum's largely stereotyped view of African Americans was changed through his working relationship with the younger and more liberal Guy Johnson. Johnson also had more recent sociology training than Odum; thus, the second folksong volume, which contained more of Johnson's input, is a much more objective study of African American song. A comparison of the two collections shows that Johnson, in this case, mentored his older colleague by changing Odum's approach to folk material.

Probably Odum's most interesting and important achievement in the field of folklore is found in his fictional trilogy about Black Ulysses. The trilogy is Odum's attempt at writing an American epic in prose and song with a black construction worker as the hero. Much of the trilogy is based on the life of John Wesley "Left Wing" Gordon, one of Odum's black informants, and the three books are a showcase for authentic Southern folklore, including traditional black expressive forms, such as signifying and bragging speeches, and common folklore genres, including tall tales, ghost tales, trickster tales, Marster and John tales, rhymes, hoodoo, and superstitions.

Odum's use of folklore varies in each of the books in the trilogy; in *Rainbow Round My Shoulder,* the folklore is largely transcriptions of tales, songs, and beliefs bound together by a narrative based on the life of Left Wing Gordon. Unfortunately, Odum's transcriptive use of folklore in this book had the effect of reinforcing his reader's stereotyped views of black culture, as evidenced from contemporary reviews of the book.

However, in *Wings on My Feet,* Odum, through Black Ulysses' narrative, uses folklore functionally to comment on the prejudice of whites toward blacks during and after World War I. This book is an important addition to the library of material on African American involvement in World War I. Because Odum's novel is a sympathetic first-person account of one black man's experience of the war, it compares favorably with other war memoirs, which often stereotype African Americans.

Odum was disappointed and worried by the lukewarm reception of *Wings on My Feet,* but he went on to use folklore functionally again in *Cold Blue Moon* to criticize racism in the South. He accomplishes his purpose of using folklore to express the need for social reform by distancing himself and his readers from these criticisms. The final book is set on a ruined antebellum plantation, and Odum comments on racial injustice through the device of folk ghost tales. The influence of his informant, Left Wing Gordon, becomes clearer as each of these books progresses, and in the last novel, Odum credits Gordon as the source of his folk material.

A careful examination of the three folk novels reveals Odum's increasing empathy for the plight of African Americans, a very different attitude from the "Christian sympathy" we see in his early sociological work. Again, the novels provide evidence that Odum's informant, Left Wing Gordon, served as a mentor who guided the folklore collector along a personal journey of enlightenment on issues of race and culture in America. It is evident that Odum made personal progress in achieving more liberal racial views if we compare his early sociological publications, such as *Social and Mental Traits of the Negro* (1910), to his folk-song studies and, finally, to his folklore trilogy. It is also clear that fiction was a good outlet for Odum's ideas because here he could showcase the folklore that he admired and use it to criticize the South he loved without facing the public disapproval aroused by more "scientific" studies. Thus, Odum's fictional trilogy, despite its faults and the obvious drawback that he recognized–that he was a white man trying to write a black man's epic–was an important step toward his better understanding of African American culture.

Odum's folklore work was also influential to a new generation of Southern liberals at the University of North Carolina, including William Terry Couch, Guy B. Johnson, and Paul Green. For example, the university press, under the direction of Couch, published many folklore manuscripts at Odum's suggestion and established a tradition of interest in folklore research that continues today.

Guy B. Johnson, Odum's student and colleague, after completing the folksong studies with Odum, went on to publish *John Henry: Tracking Down a Negro Legend* (1929), the first book devoted to the study of a single American folk song. Johnson's work is particularly important for its development of the legend of John Henry and its description of contexts in black culture for the dissemination of songs and stories about John Henry. Johnson's book also has qualities not found in his joint work with Odum, including a careful documentation of sources, variants of song texts and tunes, a discussion of the performance contexts of songs, and a more objective tone. Johnson also published *Folk Culture on St. Helena Island, S.C.* (1930), in which he discusses the speech, music, and tales of the Sea Islanders. Johnson's folklore studies are more "modern" than those of his mentor because his method of collection and analysis is more scientific than Odum's and he pays more attention to the musical qualities of folk songs.

Paul Green, another younger faculty member at the University of North Carolina, was also Odum's friend and protégé. Green, who was both a folklorist and a playwright, used folklore functionally in his plays to comment on many of the social problems that concerned Odum. Some of the songs in Green's plays came from Odum and Johnson's folk-song collections, and he used these songs and other folk material to call for social reform in the South, particularly in the areas of conservative religion and race relations.

Green, like Johnson and Couch, was one of the new generation of Southern liberals. These three members of the University of North Carolina community were younger than Odum and benefited from his experience and his trailblazing in the fields of sociology and folklore. They also took Odum's work a step further: Couch was more willing than Odum to publish "radical" material; Johnson's folklore research was more objective and scientific than Odum's; and Paul Green used folklore and social themes with greater literary success in his folk plays than did Odum in his folklore novels. These younger men expanded on Odum's ideas, but the task of discovering solutions to the problems, which Odum recognized and which they explored, was finally left to a new generation of scholars who were influenced by Odum's liberal agenda.

Odum encouraged his two sons to work in the field of ecology because he felt that subsequent progress in the South must come from a more scientific study of the land and its people and their interaction. Eugene Odum's biographer, Betty Jean Craige, notes that Howard Odum

> taught his sons how to think in terms of the larger system, how to motivate groups of individuals to address problems, how to obtain federal and private grants for university research and service, and how to persist regardless of opposition. He showed them the power of writing. He

steeped them in "liberal progressivism" and made them, like himself, crusaders for a better world. (9)

Perhaps Odum would have been disappointed at the results of scientific and industrial progress in the South, but it seems likely that he would have been pleased both with the endurance of folk traditions in the face of "development" and with his continuing influence on folklore studies at the University of North Carolina.

## Cultural Collaboration: Odum's Personal Legacy

In many ways, Southern intellectual history in the twentieth century is the story of the struggle for greater racial tolerance and cultural understanding. Howard Washington Odum's life story provides a specific example of the ways in which academic mentoring and folklore collaboration aided in one man's journey toward true racial understanding, even empathy. Odum's intellectual and emotional odyssey provides an example—for historians, and for all of us—of the transformative power of human relationships: as his student, Guy Johnson changed Odum's approach to the study of folklore, and his informant John Wesley Gordon changed his views on race. Although Odum always claimed to be a sociologist, his interest in folklore studies provided him with the key to racial understanding because it required that he abandon traditional academic hierarchy and collaborate with colleagues and informants. The interdisciplinary nature of folklore studies was also appealing to Odum because it allowed him to indulge his original humanities bent and interest in literature. Thus, Howard Odum's story not only provides insight into the ways that folklore changed the folklorist; it also tells students of Southern studies a great deal about the development of Southern history and literature.

The type of academic mentoring that Howard Odum practiced with young scholars is based on a long tradition of such relationships within both European and American universities, although Odum's approach was somewhat novel because it was more collaborative than such relationships usually are within the academy. Collaboration with folklore and ethnographic informants, however, has a more ethically ambiguous history.[1] Early collectors with humanities backgrounds, such as Child and Sharp, tended to focus more on texts than on the human beings who knew the songs or stories. Odum was also primarily interested in textual studies in folklore, but his sociology background gave his work a cultural focus as well. Thus, in some ways his work has much in common with that of contemporary folklorists. Although a complete examination of the history of folklore studies in the United States is not within the purview of this book, a brief look at recent trends in anthropology and folklore can give important insights into Odum's legacy.

Currently, anthropologists and folklorists are grappling seriously with the complexities of collector-informant relationships and the nature of collaborative ethnography. A number of fiction writers, especially those with multi-ethnic backgrounds, are also finding ways to represent multiple voices within a work. Although Odum was neither a trained folklorist nor a professional writer of fiction, his folk-song collections and folk-novel trilogy are groundbreaking in terms of his experiments with memoir, collaborative texts, and multiple voices in fiction. When we examine his folklore work in light of current theories of collaboration and polyphonic writing, Odum was clearly ahead of his time.

### Fieldwork Memoirs

During the twentieth century, anthropologists and folklorists have become increasingly interested in self-reflection and issues of identification in folklife studies, what anthropologists call ethnography, "the descriptive study of all traditions of a particular group or region" (Brunvand, *The Study of American Folklore* 406). Odum did not write ethnographies per se because he concentrated on only one aspect of culture in his folk-song collections, and his folk novels are fiction. He did, however, include autobiographical comments in his collections, and he essentially served as ghostwriter for an African American man's war memoir. Thus, looking at historical precedents for presenting personal material in anthropology and folklore can illuminate Odum's folklore and fiction.

Anthropologist Barbara Tedlock provides a good overview of the history of autobiography and memoir in ethnographies. In "From Participant Observation to the Observation of Participation: The Emergence of Narrative Ethnography" (1991), she describes early participant-observer fieldwork and responses to it from critics who felt such an approach would interfere with the scientific objectivity of the study. Tedlock explains that one common solution to the problem was "to publish the fieldwork experience as a novel" (72). She mentions the memoirs of Margaret Field (*Stormy Dawn* 1947), Laura Bohannan (*Return to Laughter* 1954), and Philip Drucker (*Tropical Frontier* 1969), which were all published under pseudonyms, as examples of ethnographic novels. The author speculates that "individuals felt that publishing a personal fieldwork account would somehow damage their reputations or credibility as professional ethnographers" (72).

Tedlock's article continues with a history of autobiographical and novelistic writing in anthropology. She explains that "in spite of its appeal, first-person, experiential writing by ethnographers dealing with actual people and events was rare during the 1930s, 1940s, and early 1950s" but that such writing became more common in the 1960s and 1970s (74, 76). Generally, however, these accounts were separated from the ethnographies themselves; Tedlock believes that this "segmentation, as in the earlier case of ethnographic novels, reveals a dualistic approach: public versus private, objective versus subjective realms of experience" (76). She goes on to note the shift in the 1970s from participant observation to the observation of participation and the number of current fieldworkers who combine "ethnographic information with a dialectic of personal involvement" (78, 79). Tedlock cites two examples—Whitehead and Conaway's *Self, Sex, and Gender in Cross-Cultural Fieldwork* (1986) and Altorki and El-Solh's *Arab Women in the Field: Studying Your Own Society* (1988)—as works that examine "the impact of an ethnographer's sex and gender identity on fieldwork and the effect of fieldwork on an ethnographer's view of gender self-identity" (79). A list of other writers who combine ethnography with personal accounts could include Lila Abu-Lughod, Michael Angrosino, Jennifer Fox, Debora Kodish, Eva Moreno, and Renato Rosaldo. Tedlock concludes her article by expressing her concern that

> the movement from ethnographic memoir to narrative ethnography has gone unanalyzed within the rapidly growing meta-anthropological literature. This omission has occurred, I think, because so much emphasis has been placed on rhetorical strategies, while substantially less attention has been given to the widening of the audience for ethnography. If today's ethnographers are writing not only for various academic audiences (area specialists, members of other disciplines, and students) but also for the educated public, including members of their host communities, then they are no longer in a position to write as if they themselves were the only active parties in cross-cultural exchanges. (81)

Tedlock's discussion is pertinent to Odum's work. First, as she notes, personal ethnographic writing was rare in Odum's day; his folk-song collections and folk-novel trilogy are very early examples of published semi-autobiographical fieldwork. Odum and Johnson use the first person frequently in the two folk-song collections to describe their fieldwork techniques. As chapter 2 makes clear, they are also not at all reticent in sharing their opinions about the artistry of various singers or the social and moral implications of the songs they collected. Although Odum only uses the first person when quoting from Gordon in the novels, much of the material in both *Rainbow Round My Shoulder* and *Cold Blue Moon* describes Odum's observations and commentary on African American culture.

Unlike ethnographic novelists who felt compelled to write under pseudonyms, Odum acknowledged the authorship of both his scholarly work and his fiction. Perhaps Odum's early background in the humanities prevented him from being self-conscious about writing fiction as well as academic studies. In fact, as noted in chapter 4, writing fiction allowed Odum to voice controversial opinions about race. The case of authorship is somewhat confused, however, when we examine Odum's novels, because as chapter 4 explains, much of the material is essentially John Wesley Gordon's memoirs as transcribed by Odum.

Finally, Tedlock's comments about recent narrative ethnographies that examine fieldworker perspectives on such issues as gender and the influence of personal and political views on ethnography are germane to an assessment of Odum's work. Although Odum does not personally reflect on his racial views in his folklore and fiction, his changing political and social views are clearly evident in his work.

In many ways, Odum became the vulnerable observer that Ruth Behar celebrates in her book *The Vulnerable Observer: Anthropology That Breaks Your Heart* (1996) because he participated in a shift that she finds only recently in anthropology, "the shift toward viewing identification, rather than difference, as the key defining image of anthropological theory and practice" (28). Ultimately Odum does identify with his informant, Left Wing Gordon, and, in fact, presents him in fiction as an Everyman figure, representative of all humanity.

Along with the shift in anthropology during the 1970s from participant observation to the observation of participation that Tedlock describes came an emphasis on performance theory in folklore. An approach that is "event-centered" rather than item- or text-centered, performance studies (also called the communication or contextual approach) focuses on folklore as artistic communication that occurs in a social context. Folklorists Roger Abrahams, Dan Ben-Amos, Richard Bauman, Elizabeth Fine, and Dell Hymes have all authored major studies utilizing the performance approach to folk material.

Odum's work anticipated the focus on performance among more recent folklorists. His theory of folklore emphasized the importance of "process," and his discussions of the origins of blues also examine the process of artistic creation. In many ways, Odum and Johnson's focus on the social function of African American folk song anticipates this later school of thought, although their approach was still more text-centered than event-centered.

## *The Ethics of Collaborative Texts*

Accurately representing the collaborative nature of folklore and ethnographic collecting has become an important issue during the past two
decades. Discussions range from topics such as ethics and avoiding
exploitation of subjects to attempts to find ways to represent dialogue
in ethnographies. Students in anthropology and folklore are reminded
to observe the ethical guidelines for collecting published by the American Folklore Society and the American Anthropological Association
on their respective Web sites. Contemporary notions of collaboration
are useful in assessing Odum's collaborative efforts with Left Wing
Gordon.

One article on the ethics of collaboration is "Negotiating Interpretive Differences Between Ethnographers and Subjects" (1992), by folklorist Elaine J. Lawless. The author reflects on her 1988 book on Pen-
tecostal women preachers, *Handmaidens of the Lord,* and her failure to
completely collaborate with her informants on that project. She explains that in her new book on clergywomen of different denomina-
tions she has attempted "reciprocal ethnography" (311). Lawless describes this process of collaborative ethnography:

> Thus, after life stories were recorded, transcribed, and returned to their
> owners; after interviews were conducted with individual clergywomen
> and transcribed for my study; and after sermons were recorded and tran-
> scribed and shared, *then* the clergywomen and I met on a regular basis
> to discuss their stories, their lives, their sermons, *as well as to discuss* my
> thoughts, interpretations, and conclusions about how all of those aspects
> of their lives were integrated and what their importance might be. (311)

While Lawless's new approach may represent "a utopia of plural authorship that accords to collaborators, not merely the status of independent enunciators, but that of writers" (Clifford 140), Barbara Myerhoff
describes ethnographies as mutually advantageous to both collector
and informant. In "Telling One's Story" (1980), she explains the importance of storytelling and performance for "socially marginal people,
disdained, ignored groups, individuals with what Erving Goffman calls

'spoiled identities'" (25). Myerhoff taught life-history classes and collected stories from Eastern European Jewish immigrants in California, many of whom were Holocaust survivors. Ethnography, according to Myerhoff, serves the purposes of the informant as well as the collector because "performance gives one self-definition" (25). In the case of Odum's primary informant, Left Wing Gordon, a marginalized black laborer is able to tell his story, not only to a white collector, but also to all readers of Odum's fiction.

Like Lawless, Daniel W. Patterson, in *A Tree Accurst: Bobby McMillon and Stories of Frankie Silver* (2000), acknowledges the importance of the collaborative method in current folklore studies. The book is dedicated to Bobby McMillon, who, while serving as Patterson's chief informant, is also an avid folklore collector himself. The book contains a good bit of historical background material and Patterson's careful analyses of the Frankie Silver ballad and legend. Throughout the chapters of primary material, however, Patterson includes both his own and McMillon's reflections on the meaning of the works that McMillon performs. For example, at one point Patterson applies folklorist Linda Degh's legend definition to the Frankie Silver cycle, then adds McMillon's comment on Degh's theory. This collaborative effort by Patterson and McMillon is an excellent example of the successful application of collaboration theory to folklore research.

Still, the ethics of collaboration and accurate representation present many difficulties for the folklorist/ethnographer. Kathleen Mullen Sands discusses these ethical issues at length in her book *Telling a Good One: The Process of a Native American Collaborative Biography* (2000). Sands's experience with Native storyteller Ted Rios usefully parallels Odum's work with John Wesley Gordon. Both collectors are dealing with informants from historically marginalized American ethnic groups. Although Rios and Gordon speak English, both collectors have to deal with issues of dialect and ethnic metaphor in accurately presenting the speakers' stories. Sands is reflective about these issues in a way that Odum is not, but both collectors have the goal of presenting material that will help readers understand either Native American or

African American culture within the context of American culture in general.

Early in her book, Sands addresses the criticisms of those who claim that outsider collectors of another culture are always exploitative. One such critic, Elizabeth Cook-Lynn, objects to Native American collaborative autobiography because she sees the final product as not only "stolen intellectual property" but also, according to Sands, work that can "undermine the integrity of Native American expression" and "mislead both non-Natives and Natives about Native American identity" (253). Sands agrees with Cook-Lynn that "Native American personal narratives are, in that sense, exploitive. They offer primarily non-Native readers a version of Native American personhood that may lead to a false sense of knowing Indianness" (254).

Yet Sands also finds limitations in the criticisms of colonial theory because in

> addressing collaborative life story . . . it focuses exclusively on the power balance between the two parties and deflects attention away from the actual performance of narrative. . . . Moreover, it presumes that the collaborative power balance is consistently unidirectional and tends to define narrators as victims rather than essential and usually willing partners in a dialogic enterprise. . . . Because colonial theory is a way of analyzing encounter and resultant text that generally discounts the subversive, resistant, and/or cooperative power that the narrator can . . . manifest in the oral mode of narrating life experiences, it tends to be dismissive of the Native elements of control in the life-story collaboration. (35)

Sands's recognition of the possible "subversive, resistant, and/or cooperative power" of informants is pertinent to Odum's collaboration with Gordon. Although Odum almost certainly began collecting from Gordon in the guise of a scholarly authority figure, even paying him with whiskey according to Johnson, it also seems clear that Gordon had some influence on shaping his own narrative. In his article "On Ethnographic Authority" (1983), James Clifford asserts that "indigenous control over knowledge gained in the field can be considerable, and even determining" (136).

Although it is difficult to know with any certainty in what ways Gordon shaped his own story, Odum's increasingly sympathetic and heroic portrayal of Gordon as the novels progress seems to provide evidence that Gordon may have been selective in his choice of material to share with Odum. Gordon seemingly had no qualms about telling stories about his own drunkenness, promiscuity, or violent behavior; still, he comes across in the novels as brave, strong, stoic about persecution, and loyal to friends. How much of the positive aspect of Gordon's character portrayal is due to Odum's increasing identification with his informant and how much is due to Gordon's narrative power is impossible to ascertain. As I conclude in chapter 4, however, it seems likely that some of Gordon's more subversive sentiments, such as his comment that he refuses to be a "black leaf blowed 'bout by white man in some dam' fence corner" (*Cold Blue Moon* 268), are direct quotes. If nothing else, Odum's increasingly liberal tone on issues of race in his work seems directly attributable to Gordon's influence.

## *Presentation Styles for Collaborative Texts*

An issue that has dominated literary criticism during the past decades, the nature of discourse, has also become the focus of much recent work in anthropology. Scholars in both fields typically refer to the work of the influential Russian critic Mikhail Bakhtin and his discussion of the "polyphonic" novel (430–31). According to Bakhtin, language is "dialogic" or conversational; the best writers, such as Dickens and Dostoevsky, are able to represent this quality of language in their fiction. Several folklore and anthropology scholars have applied Bakhtin's ideas to the study of culture; their ideas provide some useful insights into Odum's experimental folk novels.

Odum's narratives reflect his attempts to accurately represent the nature of Left Wing Gordon's various levels of discourse. In "Rethinking

Moral Responsibility in Fieldwork: The Situated Negotiation of Research Ethics in Anthropology and Sociology" (1991), William Graves III and Mark A. Shields comment that "Bakhtin's conception of social life as a 'polyphony of voices'" is valuable to discussions of ethics and collaboration in fieldwork "because of its insistence on the importance of accommodating multiple perspectives without reducing the complex 'dialogic' fabric of social life to a uniform, 'monologic,' authoritarian explanation" (148). In his first and third novels, Odum represents his dialogue with Gordon by formally separating their Standard English and Black English voices. However, as the analysis in chapter 4 suggests, his technique in *Wings on My Feet* is more sophisticated and ultimately more "dialogic."

Elaine Lawless notes that she has "given up the notion of scholar voice as privileged voice, the scholar's position as more legitimate because it is the more educated or more credible one." Still, she believes that "the feminist scholar looking at an oppressive situation for women has both the right and the obligation to point out that the situation *is* oppressive, and that the women involved may justifiably fear repercussions for their actions" (312). Like Lawless, as Odum increasingly collaborated with his primary informant, he looked for ways to best represent Left Wing Gordon's voice, but he also felt a scholar's obligation to comment on his African American friend's position in a racist world.

Odum's three folk novels are also "polyphonic" in Bakhtin's sense of the term. In "On Ethnographic Authority," James Clifford notes that "with expanded communication and intercultural influence, people interpret others, and themselves, in a bewildering diversity of idioms—a global condition of what Bakhtin called 'heteroglossia'" (119). Clifford compares this interaction to the "polyphonic" novel discussed by Bakhtin and notes that Bakhtin's ideal novelist is a ventriloquist or "polyphonist" (136–37). In his article, Clifford examines ethnographic presentation style, commenting that both novelists and anthropologists can use one of two approaches, free indirect style, which "suppresses direct quotation in favor of a controlling discourse always more-or-less that of the author," or an approach that is "stylistically less homogeneous" and "filled with . . . 'different voices.'" Clifford comments that "some use of indirect style is inevitable, unless the novel or ethnography be composed entirely of quotations, which is theoretically possible but seldom attempted" (137). Clifford sees resistance to polyphonic ethnography, however, because "the very idea of plural authorship challenges a deep Western identification of any text's order with the intention of a single author" (140).

Interestingly, Odum's approach to presenting his fieldwork in fictional form is exactly the one that Clifford claims is unusual; his novels consist almost entirely of quotations from his informant. In *Rainbow Round My Shoulder* and *Cold Blue Moon,* Odum does indeed try to shape Left Wing Gordon's narrative by introducing each chapter with his own prose, but as noted in chapter 4, this technique is less successful from a literary point of view and less convincing from a folklore point of view than the one he uses in *Wings on My Feet,* where the entire novel consists of quotations.

Kathleen Sands notes that what Western readers expect of personal narrative is "a comprehensive and continuous narrative in chronological order," but because of the "collaborative nature of Native American orally narrated life story, forcing it into a Euro-American literary genre wrests the narrative out of the cross-cultural process from which it has been generated" (3). Odum tells Gordon's African American narrative chronologically, but his presentation of Gordon's story still has many cross-cultural elements. In some ways, Odum's novel style anticipates that of African American author Toni Morrison.

In a 1984 interview, Morrison commented that an important aspect of African American art is its

> ability to be both print and oral literature: to combine those two aspects so that the stories can be read in silence, of course, but one should be able to hear them as well. . . . To make the story appear oral, meandering, effortless, spoken– . . . to have the reader work *with* the author in the construction of the book–is what's important. (qtd. in Harris 1)

Trudier Harris opens her book *Fiction and Folklore: The Novels of Toni Morrison* (1991) with this quotation, and proceeds to discuss the many ways that Morrison uses folklore to achieve this immediate oral quality in her fiction. For Harris, Morrison's "saturation" in traditional African American culture allows her to use folklore naturally, gracefully, and organically to enhance her fiction. One technique that Harris describes is Morrison's narrative approach in the novel *Beloved* (1987), in which she develops "her novel associatively, that is, by narratively duplicating the patterns of the mind, the way it gathers tidbits of experiences in *seemingly* random fashion, she achieves a structural effect that evokes the process of oral narration" (172).

While Howard Odum was not immersed in African American culture, his informant, Left Wing Gordon, was. By resisting the impulse to control and shape Gordon's story for him, especially in *Wings on My Feet,* Odum was able to approach the oral quality that Harris finds in Morrison's novels. While Odum's fiction does not achieve the transcendence of Morrison's, his willingness to experiment with the fictional presentation of folk material is remarkable.

Odum's use of orality in fiction is a testament to his understanding of African American culture and his empathy with Left Wing Gordon. If oral qualities in print literature represent something fundamental about African American art, then Odum's novels are truly a collaboration between a black artist and a white transcriber. In political terms, Odum's work is not only less racist than the other World War I memoirs described in chapter 4, his novels are also much less exploitative than the many recent collaborative biographies and autobiographies focusing on Native Americans and other racial, ethnic, and cultural groups.

Finally, the most useful idea for assessing Odum's contribution to the field of collaborative texts is Clifford's comment about reader-response theory, which "suggests that the ability of a text to make sense in a coherent way depends less on the willed intentions of an originating author than on the creative activity of a reader" (141). If readers find the voice of Left Wing Gordon believable and his story enlightening, then Odum's fiction is worthy of renewed attention.

Ultimately, the most important aspect of Odum's experiments with collaboration may be the way it changed his own life. In "Telling One's Story," Barbara Myerhoff writes: "How a tale is heard and how profoundly it affects the one who hears it as well as the one who tells it is an important theme in my work." She continues by describing an informant who refuses to tell his life story because, he says, "If I tell you my life story, and if you really listen, you will be changed. What right have I to do that to you? On the other hand, if I tell you my life story, and if you really listen, and you are not changed, why should I bother?" (28–29). Hearing and recording John Wesley Gordon's story certainly changed Howard Odum; the story of that change can provide insights into the history of race relations in America.

## Conclusion

The story of Howard W. Odum's development as a folklorist and Southern intellectual is a story of mentoring. Like many educators, both then and today, Odum devoted his life to work that would fulfill the call to Christian service that he learned from his parents. He was subsequently influenced by teachers who believed that science could solve America's social problems. Luckily, Odum's interest in serving society led him to African American folk song as a source of cultural information, and he was necessarily influenced by his adopted discipline.

Howard Odum's story is also one about the art of collaboration. Odum took the unusual step of collaborating on two folk-song collections with his student Guy Johnson, who was listed as coauthor and served as not only editor but contributor, especially to the second collection, *Negro Workaday Songs*. In addition, Odum collaborated with his informant, John Wesley "Left Wing" Gordon, and wrote three folk novels based on the oral memoirs of Gordon's life.

Odum never claimed to be a folklorist, but it is clear that is what he became. Because he was willing to abandon academic hierarchy and collaborate with his student Guy Johnson, he learned about cutting-edge approaches to folk material practiced by anthropologists at the time. Because he was willing to see Left Wing Gordon as an artist, he learned about black culture firsthand and was able to publish one of the most complete collections of African American folklore from the early part of the twentieth century. Because Odum became a folklorist, his views on race changed, and his story provides us with an example of the effectiveness of collaboration and individual friendship.

Perhaps Odum was attracted to folk studies because he saw the limitations of a completely scientific approach to race relations. His background in both practical Christianity and the classics helped him appreciate the role of individuals in effecting changes in society. Clearly, he was also touched by the artistry of black folk music. At first it seems that publishing in the field of folklore was expedient for him, but eventually Odum recognized both the value of the material he collected and his own limitations as an outsider to the culture he examined. Ultimately, in the folk trilogy, he allowed his informant to speak in his own words, and thus provided a rare forum for a black man in Depression-era America. Thus, Odum's willingness to both mentor and be mentored seems to be the clue to his development as a folklorist and to his changing views on race.

In addition, the lives of contemporary Southerners have been positively influenced by Howard Washington Odum's remarkable contributions to racial understanding. While most Americans agree that we still have a long road ahead to achieve true racial tolerance, Howard Odum's life is a lesson in how to reach that goal. Perhaps a few people learn about other human beings from books; most of us change our perceptions of others only when we become close to individual human beings, in friendship and in love. Howard Odum became friends with Guy Johnson and John Wesley Gordon and grew to love and understand them. The South of my childhood and adult life is a far more multicultural and tolerant place than it was in Odum's youth, and the change is a result of his influence. Just as my academic career has been influenced by my various mentoring experiences, it has also been influenced positively by my research on Odum's life. "I am a part of all that I have met" seems an appropriate epigram for Howard Odum's life and for those of us whose lives have been changed by his ideas.

# Notes

*Preface*

1. For a bibliography of Odum's publications, see *Folk, Region, and Society.*

*One. African American Folklore and Odum's Liberal Agenda at the University of North Carolina*

1. For an overview of the topic, see D. K. Wilgus's chapter on the spiritual in *Anglo-American Folksong Scholarship since 1898* (1959).

*Two. Odum and Johnson's Collaborative Folk-Song Collections*

1. Although the phonograph was first used for fieldwork in 1890 when Fewkes recorded Passamaquoddy Indians in Maine, folklorists were slow to adopt recording machines. Frank C. Brown had a cylinder machine by 1915; R. W. Gordon recorded with one in North Carolina in 1925. In an interview, Johnson discussed his failed attempts with the Ediphone during his Sea Island research. The machine recorded on wax cylinders, which subsequently melted in Johnson's attic during the hot Chapel Hill summer. Johnson donated these cylinders to the Southern Folklife Collection at the University of North Carolina, where archivists are currently working to restore them. Odum, like most researchers in the 1920s and earlier, recorded his notes with pencil and paper, obviously an inexact method for collecting music.

*Five. Folklore and Racial Tolerance in the Academy*

1. Published in *The Lord's Will and Other Carolina Plays* (1925).
2. Published in *In the Valley and Other Carolina Plays* (1928).
3. Published in *Lonesome Road: Six Plays for the Negro Theatre* (1926).
4. *The End of the Row* was published in *Lonesome Road* (1926). *The Goodbye* was published in *In the Valley* (1928).

5. The play is a reworking of two earlier one-act plays, *In Abraham's Bosom* and *Your Fiery Furnace,* both published in *Lonesome Road* (1926).

## Six. Mentoring and Collaboration as Keys to Cultural Understanding

1. Among the ethical topics concerning folklorists and anthropologists to-day is the use of the term "informant." Although I am aware of the negative implications of the term and the preference of many ethnographers for the term "collaborator," it has seemed necessary to use "informant" in reference to John Wesley Gordon in this book in order to adequately illuminate Odum's unusual attitude toward collaboration.

# Works Cited

References to the Howard Washington Odum Papers and the Paul Green Papers, in the Southern Historical Collection, University of North Carolina Library, Chapel Hill, are abbreviated *Odum Papers* and *Green Papers, UNC,* respectively.

## Works by Howard Washington Odum

*For a complete bibliography of Odum's publications, see the last item in this list.*

"Religious Folk-songs of Southern Negroes." *American Journal of Religious Psychology and Education* 3 (July 1909): 265–365.

*Social and Mental Traits of the Negro.* New York: Columbia University Press, 1910.

"Folk-Song and Folk-Poetry: As Found in the Secular Songs of the Southern Negroes." *Journal of American Folklore* 24, no. 93 (1911): 255–94.

"Folk-song and Folk-poetry: As Found in the Secular Songs of the Southern Negroes." *Journal of American Folklore* 24, no. 94 (1911): 351–96.

"Negro Hymns." *Journal of American Folklore* 26 (1913): 376.

Letter to Albert Bushnell Hart, March 20, 1920. Odum Papers, UNC.

Letter to Harry Woodburn Chase, May 3, 1920. Odum Papers, UNC.

Letter to W. W. Alexander, July 19, 1921. Odum Papers, UNC.

Suggestions with Reference to Black Ulysses Singing. Odum Papers, UNC. N.d., probably mid-1920s.

Letter to Miss Cecile Phillips, December 5, 1927. Odum Papers, UNC.

*Rainbow Round My Shoulder: The Blue Trail of Black Ulysses.* Indianapolis: Bobbs-Merrill, 1928.

Customs House letter and attached note, November 8, 1929. Odum Papers, UNC.

*Wings on My Feet: Black Ulysses at the Wars.* Indianapolis: Bobbs-Merrill, 1929.

Letter to D. L. Chambers, January 21, 1930. Odum Papers, UNC.

Letter to D. L. Chambers, February 18, 1930. Odum Papers, UNC.

*Cold Blue Moon: Black Ulysses Afar Off.* Indianapolis: Bobbs-Merrill, 1931.

Black Rainbow, Random Notes on MS for *Wings on My Feet.* Odum Papers, UNC. March 23, 1934.

*Southern Regions of the United States.* Chapel Hill: University of North Carolina Press, 1936.

Tentative Memorandum: Regional and Folk Portraiture as Materials for Social Science. Odum Papers, UNC. N.d., probably 1930s.

On Trying to Define the Field and Methods of a Dynamic Folk Sociology. Work Memorandum. March 1947. Odum Papers, UNC.

"On Southern Literature and Southern Culture." In *Southern Renascence: The Literature of the Modern South.* Ed. Louis D. Rubin Jr. and Robert D. Jacobs. Baltimore: Johns Hopkins University Press, 1953.

*Folk, Region, and Society: Selected Papers of Howard W. Odum.* Chapel Hill: University of North Carolina Press, 1964.

## Other Works Cited

Aarne, Antti Amatus. *The Types of the Folktale: A Classification and Bibliography.* Translated and enlarged by Stith Thompson. Helsinki: Suomalainen Tiedeakatemia, 1961.

Abrahams, Roger. *Talking Black.* Rowley, Mass.: Newbury House, 1976.

Adams, Agatha. *Paul Green of Chapel Hill.* Chapel Hill: University of North Carolina Library, 1951.

Allen, William Francis, Charles Pickard Ware, and Lucy McKim Garrison. *Slave Songs of the United States.* New York: Peter Smith, 1867.

*American Folklore: An Encyclopedia.* Ed. Jan Harold Brunvand. New York: Garland, 1996.

Austin, Mary. Review of *Rainbow Round My Shoulder,* by Howard Odum. *Saturday Review of Literature* 4 (April 21, 1928): 778–79.

Bakhtin, M. M. *The Dialogic Imagination.* Ed. Michael Holquist. Trans. Caryl Emerson and Michael Holquist. Austin: University of Texas Press, 1981.

Behar, Ruth. *The Vulnerable Observer: Anthropology That Breaks Your Heart.* Boston: Beacon, 1996.

Brazil, Wayne Douglas. *Howard W. Odum: The Building Years, 1884–1930.* New York: Garland, 1988.

Bronner, Simon. *American Folklore Studies: An Intellectual History.* Lawrence: University Press of Kansas, 1986.

Brunvand, Jan Harold. *The Study of American Folklore.* 4th ed. New York: Norton, 1998.

Bulmer, Martin. *The Chicago School of Sociology.* Chicago: University of Chicago Press, 1984.

Cade, John Brother. *Twenty-Two Months with "Uncle Sam": Being the Experiences and Observations of a Negro Student Who Volunteered for Military Service Against the Central Powers from June, 1917 to April, 1919.* Atlanta: Robinson-Cofer Company Printers, 1929.

Carter, Isabel Gordon. Review of *The Negro and His Songs,* by Guy B. Johnson and Howard W. Odum. *Journal of American Folklore* 38, no. 150 (1925): 623–24.

Chambers, D. L. Letter to Howard Odum, April 14, 1930. Odum Papers, UNC.

Chappell, Louis W. *John Henry: A Folklore Study.* Jena, Frommannsche Verlag: Walter Biedermann, 1933.

Clifford, James. "On Ethnographic Authority." *Representations* 1, no. 2 (1983): 118–46.

Cohen, Hennig. "American Literature and American Folklore." In *Our Living Traditions.* Ed. Tristram P. Coffin. New York: Basic Books, 1968. 238–47.

*Complete History of the Colored Soldiers in the World War.* New York: Bennett and Churchill, 1919.

Conway, Cecelia. *African Banjo Echoes in Appalachia: A Study of Folk Traditions.* Knoxville: University of Tennessee Press, 1995.

Craige, Betty Jean. *Eugene Odum: Ecosystem Ecologist and Environmentalist.* Athens: University of Georgia Press, 2001.

Daniels, Jonathan. Review of *Cold Blue Moon,* by Howard Odum. *Saturday Review of Literature* 7 (April 25, 1931): 774.

Davidson, Donald. *The Attack on Leviathan: Regionalism and Nationalism in the United States.* Chapel Hill: University of North Carolina Press, 1938.

Dorson, Richard. *Negro Folktales in Michigan.* Westport, Conn.: Greenwood Press, 1956.

Evans, David. *Big Road Blues: Tradition and Creativity in Folk Blues.* Berkeley: University of California Press, 1982.

Faulkner, William. *Sartoris.* New York: Random House, 1929.

————. *The Wishing Tree.* New York: Random House, 1964.

Fenton, Joan. "Howard Cotton: A Black Teller of Tall Tales." M.A. thesis, University of North Carolina, 1981.

Graves, William, III, and Mark A. Shields. "Rethinking Moral Responsibility in Fieldwork: The Situated Negotiation of Research Ethics in Anthropology and Sociology." In *Ethics and the Profession of Anthropology: Dialogue for a New Era.* Ed. Carolyn Fluehr-Lobban. Philadelphia: University of Pennsylvania Press, 1991.

Green, Paul. *The Hawthorn Tree.* Chapel Hill: University of North Carolina Press, 1943.

————. *In Abraham's Bosom and The Field God.* New York: Robert McBride, 1926, 1927.

————. *In the Valley and Other Carolina Plays.* New York: Samuel French, 1928.

————. Letter from Howard Odum, July 1, 1925. Green Papers, UNC.

————. Letter from Howard Odum, August 6, 1930. Green Papers, UNC.

————. Letter to Howard Odum, January 21, 1925. Green Papers, UNC.

————. Letter to Howard Odum, January 14, 1928. Green Papers, UNC.

————. Letter to Howard Odum, September 11, 1933. Green Papers, UNC.

————. *Lonesome Road: Six Plays for the Negro Theatre.* New York: Robert McBride, 1926.

————. *The Lord's Will and Other Carolina Plays.* New York: Henry Holt, 1925.

————. *Roll, Sweet Chariot: A Symphonic Play for the Negro People.* New York: Samuel French, 1935.

————. *Words and Ways: Stories and Incidents from My Cape Fear Valley Folklore Collection.* Raleigh: North Carolina Folklore Society, 1968.

Harris, Joel Chandler. *Uncle Remus.* New York: Appleton, 1895.

Harris, Trudier. *Fiction and Folklore: The Novels of Toni Morrison.* Knoxville: University of Tennessee Press, 1991.

Hemenway, Robert. *Zora Neale Hurston: A Literary Biography.* Chicago: University of Illinois Press, 1977.

Hobson, Fred. *Tell About the South: The Southern Rage to Explain.* Baton Rouge: Louisiana State University Press, 1983.

Hurston, Zora Neale. *Mules and Men.* 1935. Reprint, New York: Harper and Row, Perennial Library, 1990.

Jackson, Bruce. *The Negro and His Folklore in Nineteenth-Century Periodicals.* Austin: University of Texas Press, 1967.

Jackson, George Pullen. *White and Negro Spirituals.* 1943. Reprint, New York: Da Capo Press, 1975.

Johnson, Charles S. Letter to Howard Odum, January 4, 1928. Odum Papers, UNC.

Johnson, Gerald. Letter to Howard Odum, January 9, 1928. Odum Papers, UNC.

Johnson, Guion Griffis, and Guy Benton Johnson. *Research in Service to Society: The First Fifty Years of the IRSS at the University of North Carolina.* Chapel Hill: University of North Carolina Press, 1980.

Johnson, Guy Benton. *Folk Culture on St. Helena Island.* Chapel Hill: University of North Carolina Press, 1930.

————. "Howard Washington Odum: An Appreciation." *Phylon* 16, no. 1 (1955): 102.

————. *John Henry: Tracking Down a Negro Legend.* Chapel Hill: University of North Carolina Press, 1929.

————. *My Love Affair with Music and Other Personal Recollections.* Chapel Hill: Institute for Research in Social Science and the Department of Sociology, 1986.

————. Personal interview. February 6, 1985. Chapel Hill, N.C.

————. Telephone interview. October 6, 1986. Chapel Hill, N.C.

Johnson, Guy Benton, and Howard W. Odum. *The Negro and His Songs: A Study of Typical Songs in the South.* Chapel Hill: University of North Carolina Press, 1925.

————. *Negro Workaday Songs.* Chapel Hill: University of North Carolina Press, 1926.

Joyner, Charles. *Down by the Riverside: A South Carolina Slave Community.* Urbana: University of Illinois Press, 1984.

Kennedy, Emmett. Review of *Wings on My Feet,* by Howard Odum. *Saturday Review of Literature* 6 (October 12, 1929): 244.

Kenny, Vincent. *Paul Green.* New York: Twayne, 1971.

Koch, Frederick. Introduction to *Carolina Playmakers: First Series.* New York: Henry Holt, 1922.

Lawless, Elaine J. " 'I was afraid someone like you . . . an outsider . . . would misunderstand': Negotiating Interpretive Differences Between Ethnographers and Subjects." *Journal of American Folklore* 105, no. 417 (1992): 302–14.

Levy, M. P. Review of *Rainbow Round My Shoulder,* by Howard Odum. *The New Republic* 56 (September 26, 1928): 159.

Lewis, Nell Battle. Review of *The Negro and His Songs,* by Guy B. Johnson and Howard W. Odum. *North Carolina Historical Review* 2, nos. 1–4 (1925): 541–43.

Linney, Daniel. "Social Problems in the Plays of Paul Green." Thesis, University of North Carolina, 1964.

MacIntyre, W. Irwin. *Colored Soldiers.* Macon, Georgia: J. W. Burke, 1923.

Mencken, H. L. Review of *Rainbow Round My Shoulder,* by Howard Odum. *American Mercury,* September 1928.

Merriam, Alan P. *The Anthropology of Music.* Northwestern University Press, 1964.

Milligan, Michael. "The 'Universal Constant in a World of Societal Variables': Howard Odum's Use of the 'Folk' Concept in Folk Sociology, 1930–1953." *The Folklore Historian* 8 (1991): 5–25.

Mims, Edward. *The Advancing South: Stories of Progress and Reaction.* New York: Doubleday, 1926.

Myerhoff, Barbara. "Telling One's Story." *The Center Magazine* 13, no. 2 (1980): 22–40.

Obituary of Howard W. Odum, *Washington Post,* November 14, 1954. Odum Papers, UNC.

Patterson, Daniel W. *A Tree Accurst: Bobby McMillon and Stories of Frankie Silver.* Chapel Hill: University of North Carolina Press, 2000.

Pearce, Howard. "From Folklore to Mythology: Paul Green's *Roll, Sweet Chariot.*" *Southern Literary Journal* 3, no. 2 (spring 1971): 62–78.

Pound, Louise. Review of *John Henry,* by Guy B. Johnson. *Journal of American Folklore* 43, no. 167 (1930): 126–27.

Puckett, Newbell Niles. *Folk Beliefs of the Southern Negro.* Chapel Hill: University of North Carolina Press, 1926.

Rios, Theodore, and Kathleen Mullen Sands. *Telling a Good One: The Process of a Native American Collaborative Biography.* Lincoln: University of Nebraska Press, 2000.

Roberts, Leonard. *South from Hell-fer-Sartin.* Berea, Kentucky: Council of Southern Mountains, 1964.

Rubin, Louis D., Jr. Introduction to *I'll Take My Stand: The South and the Agrarian Tradition,* by Twelve Southerners. Gloucester, Massachusetts: Peter Smith, 1976.

Schinhan, Mary Odum. Telephone interview. December 1985.

Sharp, Cecil. *English Folk Songs from the Southern Appalachians*. London: Oxford University Press, 1932.

Simpson, George L., Jr. "Howard W. Odum and American Regionalism." *Social Forces* 34, no. 2 (1955), 101–6.

Singal, Daniel J. *The War Within: From Victorian to Modernist Thought in the South, 1919–1945*. Chapel Hill: University of North Carolina Press, 1982.

Smitherman, Geneva. *Talkin and Testifyin: The Language of Black America*. Boston: Houghton Mifflin, 1977.

Sosna, Morton Phillip. *In Search of the Silent South*. New York: Columbia University Press, 1977.

Spearman, Walter. *The Carolina Playmakers: The First Fifty Years*. Chapel Hill: University of North Carolina Press, 1970.

Tedlock, Barbara. "From Participant Observation to the Observation of Participation: The Emergence of Narrative Ethnography." *Journal of Anthropological Research* 47, no. 1 (1991): 69–94.

Tindall, George B. *The Ethnic Southerners*. Baton Rouge: Louisiana State University Press, 1976.

———. "The Significance of Howard W. Odum to Southern History." *Journal of Southern History* 24, no. 3 (1958): 287–305.

Traugott, Elizabeth Closs, and Mary Louise Pratt. *Linguistics*. New York: Harcourt Brace Jovanovich, 1980.

Turner, Lorenzo Dow. *Africanisms in the Gullah Dialect*. Ann Arbor: University of Michigan Press, 1949.

Vance, Rupert. "Howard W. Odum and the Case of the South." Paper presented at the Southeastern Meeting of the American Studies Association, April 11, 1970.

Van Doren, Mark. Review of *Rainbow Round My Shoulder,* by Howard Odum. *The Nation* 126 (March 28, 1928): 351.

White, Newman Ivey. Review of *The Negro and His Songs,* by Guy B. Johnson and Howard W. Odum. *South Atlantic Quarterly* 24 (1925): 441–44.

———. Review of *Negro Workaday Songs,* by Guy B. Johnson and Howard W. Odum. *South Atlantic Quarterly* 25 (1926): 431–33.

Wilgus, D. K. *Anglo-American Folksong Scholarship since 1898*. New Brunswick: Rutgers University Press, 1959.

Williamson, Joel. *The Crucible of Race: Black-White Relations in the American South since Emancipation*. New York: Oxford University Press, 1984.

Wilson, Louis R. *The University of North Carolina, 1900–1930: The Making of a Modern University.* Chapel Hill: University of North Carolina Press, 1957.

Zug, Charles G. "Folklore and the Drama: The Carolina Playmakers and Their 'Folk Plays.'" *Southern Folklore Quarterly* 32, no. 4 (1968): 279–94.

Zumwalt, Rosemary. *American Folklore Scholarship: A Dialogue of Dissent.* Bloomington: Indiana University Press, 1988.

# Index

Abrahams, Roger, 66–67
*Advancing South, The* (Odum), 19
African American music. *See* music, African American
African Americans: and the chanted sermon, 32; folk expressive forms of, 66–69; folk-song scholarship of, 41–45; and the Harlem Renaissance, 48; World War I memoirs by, xii, 105–10
*African Banjo Echoes in Appalachia* (Conway), 28
*Africanisms in the Gullah Dialect* (Turner), 128
*Agenda for Integration* (Odum), 115
Agrarians, Nashville, 7–9, 17, 117
Alexander, Will, 20
*American Folklore Scholarship* (Zumwalt), 16
American Folklore Society, 16, 18
*American Journal of Religious Psychology and Education,* 10
American Sociological Society, 6
*Anglo-American Folksong Scholarship Since 1898* (Wilgus), 41, 125
animal tales, absence of, in Black Ulysses trilogy, 83–84
anthropologists, 16–17, 35, 154–57, 166
Appalachian folklore, 11, 85, 123, 159

"bad man," 44, 68, 88
Bailey, Thomas Pierce, xiii, 9–10, 149
Bakhtin, Mikhail, 161–62
ballads, 159. See also *John Henry;* Sharp, Cecil
Behar, Ruth, 157
Black English, 55, 60–66, 162
Black Ulysses trilogy, xii, 50, 51–58, 150–51; absence of animal tales in, 83–84; African American expressive forms in, 66–69; as American epic, 88–89; authenticity of boastful raps in, 67–68; *Cold Blue Moon,* 110–16; dialect in, 60–66; Everyman in, 87, 100; folklore in, 59–86; folktale genres in, 73–86; format of the novels, 87–90; race relations in, 94–95; *Rainbow Round My Shoulder,* 90–100; rap in, 67–68; rhymes, hoodoo, and beliefs in, 69–73; signifying in; 66–67; *Wings on My Feet,* 100–110
blues, ix, 35–36, 52, 91–92, 101. See *also* music, African American
Boas, Franz, 17, 18
Boggs, Ralph Steele, 16
Brazil, Wayne, ix, xi, 10, 119, 147
Bronner, Simon J., 18
Bulmer, Martin, 25

129–30; and tall tales, 51, 73–77; transcriptive, in literature, 89–90, 93, 99–100; trickster in, 88; and work songs, ix, 27, 33–34. *See also* African Americans; Gullah; music, African American

folklorists, literary, 18, 35

folk play, 8, 118, 130–44

*Folk, Region, and Society* (Odum), 7, 59

folk songs: African American scholarship of, 41–45; collections of, 11, 24–50, 122, 137, 149, 165; definition of, 35

"Folk-Song and Folk-Poetry" (Odum), 11

ghost tales, in Black Ulysses trilogy, 73, 77–81, 111–12

Gordon, John Wesley "Left Wing": collaboration of, with Odum, xiii–xiv, 55, 105–6; as Everyman, 87, 88, 157; as hero, 88, 100, 116; as informant, x, 151, 159, 161, 162, 163, 164, 165, 166; in *Negro Workaday Songs,* 37–38, 45, 51–56

Grady, Henry, 19

Graham, Frank Porter, 4

Green, Paul, xii, xiv, 8, 118; and Carolina Playmakers, 131–33; folklore in plays of, 136–38, 143–44; as folklorist, 133–35; friendship of, with Odum and Johnson, 135–36; fundamentalism in folk plays of, 138–40; and introduction to *Congaree Sketches,* 119–20; prison chain gangs in folk plays of, 142–43; race issues in folk plays of, 140–42

Gullah, 127–28, 130. *See also* Black English

Hall, G. Stanley, xiii, 2, 10, 149

Harlem Renaissance, 48. *See also* African Americans

Harris, Joel Chandler, 83, 89; and *Uncle Remus,* 27, 60–62, 100

Harris, Trudier, 163–64

Hart, Albert Bushnell, 21

Henry, John, 51, 77, 85, 88, 100, 138, 142–44

Hobson, Fred, 56

hoodoo, in Black Ulysses trilogy, 70–71

Hurston, Zora Neale, 39–40, 70–71, 77, 84, 86

Indians. *See* Native Americans

Institute for Research in Social Science (IRSS): early research at, 138, 142, 144; founding of, 4–5; Johnson and, 22, 23, 25, 29, 121; Odum and, 148, 149; publications from, 118, 119

Jackson, Bruce, 27

Jackson, George Pullen, 129–30

John Henry. *See* Henry, John

*John Henry: Tracking Down a Negro Legend* (G. B. Johnson), 5, 38, 50, 77, 118, 122–26, 151; book reviews of, 124–26

Johnson, Charles S., 98–99

Johnson, Guion Griffis, 24, 121, 127, 145

Johnson, Guy Benton: collaboration of, with Odum, xiii, xiv, 22–23, 29, 149; contributions of, to Odum's work, x, 24–26, 116,

Johnson, Guy Benton (*continued*)
166; dissertation of, 24–25; and
folk-tune transcription, 40–41;
influence of, on Odum, 25–26,
30, 45–50; sociology training of,
121–22
Johnson, James Weldon, 48
Joines, John "Frail," 85
"joreein'." *See* signifying
*Journal of American Folklore,* 11, 18,
28–29, 69
Joyner, Charles, 128

Koch, Frederick, 118, 131
Ku Klux Klan, 20, 120, 121

Lawless, Elaine J., 158–59, 162
"liberal," 2–3, 8, 9, 10, 19, 20, 131,
145, 152–53
linguistics. *See* dialect
literary folklorists, 18, 35
literary theory, 161–65; of Odum,
56–59

Marster and John tales, in Black
Ulysses trilogy, 73, 81–83
memoirs: fieldwork, of Odum,
154–57; World War I, of African
Americans, xii, 105–10
Mencken, H. L., 56, 97
mentoring, xiii, 136, 145–46, 147–53
Merriam, Alan P., 15
Milligan, Michael J., ix, 13
Mims, Edwin, 19–21
miscegenation, 140–42
Morrison, Toni, 163–64
*Motif-Index of Folk-Literature*
(Thompson), 16
*Mules and Men* (Hurston), 39–40,
70, 77, 84. *See also* Hurston, Zora
Neale

music, African American, 10, 14,
17, 22–23; blues, ix, 35–36, 52,
91–92, 101; religious songs, 12, 14,
26–27, 31–33; secular songs, 11,
26–30, 33–34, 48, 149; spirituals,
31–33, 48, 129–30
Myerhoff, Barbara, 158–59, 165

Nashville Agrarians, 7–9, 17, 117
Native Americans, 17, 159–60, 163
*Negro and His Folklore in Nineteenth-
Century Periodicals, The* (B. Jack-
son), 27
*Negro and His Songs, The* (Odum and
Johnson), 29–31, 137, 149; African
American chanted sermons in, 32;
African American religious folk
song in, 31–33; African American
secular song in, 33–34; book
reviews of, 38–39
*Negro Folktales in Michigan* (Dorson),
76, 78–79, 83
*Negro Workaday Songs* (Odum and
Johnson), 35–38, 138, 149; blues
in, 35–36; book reviews of, 39–
40; contributions of, to African
American folk-song scholarship,
41–45; definition of folk song in,
35; folklore informants in, 36–37;
Gordon in, 37, 77, 85–86, 87, 105;
John Henry in, 38, 125–26
New South movement, 19–20. *See
also* regionalism
North Carolina, 20–23, 118, 131

Odum, Eugene (son), xii, xiv,
152–53
Odum, Howard T. (son), xii, xiv
Odum, Howard W.: academic background of, 9–12; collaboration
of, with Gordon, xiii–xiv, 55,

105–6; collecting notebooks, 30, 55; contributions of, to folk-song scholarship, 41–45; and definition of "folk," 12–15; early career and education of, 2, 9–10; early fieldwork of, 10, 24, 26; family background of, 9, 148–49; as fiction writer, 24–50, 149 (*see also* Black Ulysses trilogy); folklore contributions of, 148–53; "Folk-Song and Folk-Poetry" by, 11, 27; folk-song dissertation and articles by, 10–12, 26–30; honorary degrees of, 6; influence of, on Johnson, 121–22, 127, 130; literary theory of, 56–59; obituary of, 6; "Religious Folk-Songs of Southern Negroes" by 10–11, 14; retirement of, 6; and the South of the 1920s, 19–23

*On the Trail of Negro Folksongs* (Scarborough), 16

participant observation, 155, 157
Patterson, Daniel W., 159
performance theory, 157
Puckett, Newbell Niles, 16, 69–73, 86, 110

race, 14, 19, 121, 153, 156, 161; Odum's changing views on, 23, 45, 49, 65, 87, 113–16, 146, 149, 150–51, 153, 161, 165–67
race relations: in *The Crucible of Race*, 3; ; in Odum's early research, 10–12, 14; in Paul Green's plays, 142
racism: in Black Ulysses trilogy, 56, 65, 87, 94–96, 102–4, 112, 150–51; in *The Negro and His Songs*, 32, 34; in *Negro Workaday Songs*,

x, 45, 47, 49; in the 1920s South, 19–20; and Odum's changing views, 23, 26, 52, 87, 103, 113–16, 146, 149, 161, 164, 165–67. *See also* memoirs: World War I, of African Americans
*Rainbow Round My Shoulder* (Odum), xii, 51, 59, 138, 150, 163; dialect in, 60–65; folk beliefs in, 69–71; folklore transcription in, 150; folk-song titles in, 138; and *Negro Workaday Songs,* 54; race in, 95; summary of, 90–94; tall tales in, 74–75, 84–86
Reed, John Shelton, ix
regionalism, 7–8, 14, 59, 148
religion, 92, 138–40. *See also* chanted sermon, African American; Christianity; music, African American
"Religious Folk-Songs of Southern Negroes" (Odum), 10–11, 14
*Research in Service to Society* (Johnson and Johnson), 25
Roberts, Leonard, 74, 76

Sands, Kathleen Mullen, 159–60, 163
Scarborough, Dorothy, 16
Sharp, Cecil, 11, 16, 37, 154
signifying, 66–67
Simpson, George L., 13
Singal, Daniel, xi, 25–26, 59, 116, 117–18, 145–46
*Slave Songs of the United States* (Allen, Ware, and McKim), 17
Smitherman, Geneva, 63, 66–67
*Social and Mental Traits of the Negro* (Odum), 12, 45, 95, 114, 151
*Social Forces, Journal of,* 4, 6, 24, 118, 119, 121, 139

sociology, 57–58. *See also* University
of North Carolina: Department of
Sociology
*Song Catcher in the Southern Mountains,
A* (Scarborough), 16
Sosna, Morton, 3
South, the: during the Depression,
19–23; intellectual history of,
19–23, 117–21, 147–48, 153, 165;
literature of, 57–58, 153
Southern conservative, x, 19, 22
*Southern Regions of the United States*
(Odum), ix, 5, 6–7
Southern Renaissance, 8, 56
*South from Hell-fer-Sartin* (Roberts),
74, 76
spirituals, 31–33, 48, 129–30
Stagolee, 68
St. Helena Island. See *Folk Culture on
St. Helena Island* (G. B. Johnson)

*Talking Black* (Abrahams), 66–67
tall tales, in Black Ulysses trilogy, 51,
73–77
Taylor, Archer, 16
Tedlock, Barbara, 155–57
Thompson, Stith, 16
Tindall, George, ix, 7, 15, 148
tolerance. *See* race relations
trickster, 88
Turner, Lorenzo, 128
*Types of the Folk-tale, The* (Thompson),
16, 75

*Uncle Remus* (Harris), 27, 60–62, 100
Uncle Tom stereotype, 100. *See also*
Harris, Joel Chandler

University of Chicago, 24, 25
University of Georgia, 2, 27
University of Mississippi, 2
University of North Carolina:
Department of Sociology, ix, 2,
3–4, 147; history of, 1, 5, 44, 131;
and Johnson, 24; liberalism at,
20–21; and Odum as mentor,
145–46, 147, 152, 153
University of North Carolina Press,
xii, 5, 118–21, 145

Vance, Rupert, ix, xi, 12–13

war. *See* World War I
*White and Negro Spirituals* (G.
Jackson), 129
Whitman, Walt, 88–89
Wilgus, D. K., 41, 125
Williamson, Joel, 3, 9, 146
Wilson, Louis R., 4–5, 119
*Wings on My Feet* (Odum), xii, 51,
59–60, 163; book review of, 103–
4; dialect in, 65; folk-song titles in,
86; functional use of folklore in,
90, 150; and other World War I
memoirs, 105–10; race in, 97–98;
summary of, 100–103
Woofter, T. J., Jr., 127, 145
work songs, ix, 27, 33–34
World War I, xii, 59, 100, 104, 150;
African American memoirs of, xii,
105–10. See also *Wings on My Feet*

Zug, Charles G., 131–32
Zumwalt, Rosemary, 16–17, 18